YOUR AVERAGE
NIGGA

African American Life Series

*A complete listing of the books in this series
can be found online at wsupress.wayne.edu*

Series Editors

Melba Joyce Boyd
Department of Africana Studies, Wayne State University

Ronald Brown
Department of Political Science, Wayne State University

YOUR AVERAGE NIGGA

PERFORMING RACE LITERACY AND MASCULINITY

VERSHAWN ASHANTI YOUNG

WAYNE STATE UNIVERSITY PRESS   DETROIT

Library of Congress Cataloging-in-Publication Data

Young, Vershawn Ashanti.
Your average nigga : performing race, literacy, and masculinity /
Vershawn Ashanti Young.
p. cm. — (African American life series)
Includes bibliographical references (p.) and index.
ISBN-13: 978-0-8143-3248-1 (pbk. : alk. paper)
ISBN-10: 0-8143-3248-X (pbk. : alk. paper)
1. African American men—Social conditions. 2. African Americans—
Race identity. 3. Race awareness—United States. 4. Racism—
United States. 5. Young, Vershawn Ashanti. 6. African American men—
Biography. 7. African American men—Psychology. 8. Masculinity—United
States. 9. African American men—Language. 10. Literacy—Social aspects—
United States. I. Title. II. Series.
E185.86.Y67 2007
305.38'896073—dc22
2006100156

Chapter 4 was originally published as "Your Average Nigga," *College
Composition and Communication* 55, no. 4 (2004): 693–715. Copyright 2004
by the National Council of Teachers of English. Reprinted with permission.

Chapter 2 was originally published as "So Black I'm Blue," *Minnesota
Review*, n.s., 58–60 (2003): 207–19.

Designed and typeset by Maya Rhodes
Composed in Ehrhardt MT and Helvetica

To Dorothy "Momma" Young, for giving me life and literacy,
and to the late Chicago journalist Leanita McClain (1951–1984):
May her voice continue to inspire.

Almost all Negroes . . . are almost always acting, but before a white audience—which is quite incapable of judging their performance: and even the "bad nigger" is, inevitably, giving something of a performance, even if the entire purpose of his performance is to terrify or blackmail white people.

JAMES BALDWIN, "Alas, Poor Richard"

As a middle-class black man I have often felt myself contriving to be "black."

SHELBY STEELE, *The Content of Our Character*

contents

prelude
The Barbershop

While sitting in the only black barbershop in Cedar Rapids, Iowa, on the morning of writing this prelude, trying to think of the best way to acquaint you with what this book is about and who I am as the author behind it, I was struck with just how different I am from a lot of other black men, and yet again I was compelled to acknowledge my desire to be like them. The men I observed walked with that lanky dip I wish I could perfect; they talked casually but passionately about sports, basketball especially, with the deep resonance that reverberates in my hungry ears. Many spoke a spicy black lingo, the hip linguistics that even white kids from Iowa crave. The men wore pants that sagged. Their feet were adorned with the latest two-hundred-dollar sneakers endorsed by Allen Iverson or Shaq. Their self-assurance made me want to mimic them, to give a gender performance that would say un-equivocally to everybody—white folks, black folks, everybody—that I too am a black male with balls. That's part of why *I* was at the barber-shop—and to get that fresh bald fade, one of the trendy hallmarks of black masculinity.

However, because this barbershop is located smack dab in the middle of Mostly White, Iowa—a state that unapologetically leads in incarcerating black men—my vicarious revel in black masculinity was sobered by the statistics: while only 2 percent of those who live in Iowa are black, blacks comprise 25 percent of the state's prison population.[1] Thus in addition to enchantment, I felt a conflicting fusion of fortune and tribulation—fortune because my language and demeanor often mark me as educated, separating me from those who exemplify the stigmatized (and paradoxically romanticized) black male profile, and consequently excusing me, though certainly not always, from the plight that follows that image. I am troubled because the black men who suffer most from the educational and judicial systems are poor, from the underclass, from the ghetto, like me. And although many flee the big city, looking for a small haven in mid-America, they sometimes find that their situation gets worse. I both identify with their predicament and disidentify with it because I am and am not exactly one of them, and both do and do not want to be.[2]

To embrace my blackness, my heritage, my manliness, I identify with men who represent the ghetto. I no longer want to deny my class background or the racial experience associated with it. I identify to belong. I disidentify to escape racism, to avoid the structures that oppress black men. But I also disidentify to retaliate against black men—to punish them for what I perceive as their efforts to disown me. This ambivalence provokes me to imitate and just as often to dissociate from the black men I envy. Both efforts fail. Neither alleviates my racial anxiety. Instead, they heighten the angst I experience. As a result I am hyperaware of how masculine I am (not) and how black I (don't) act.

I can't neatly explain why my visit to the barbershop brings all this to mind and spurs my unease. I mean, the barbers are only courteous. They take me ahead of clients who come less frequently. They even call me sir, although I'm not much older than they are and tell them to use my first name. Still, I can't shake the way I feel. For although I know that some of my discomfort is self-induced, a consequence of not conversing much with the barbers and their customers about their racial and gender performances and not allowing them to give their take on mine, I also know there's reason for my worry, that my experience is not unique.[3]

Shelly Eversley aptly summarizes part of the reason for my concern in her book *The Real Negro*.[4] Offering an anecdote about the time she felt uncomfortable in a black barbershop in Baltimore, Eversley concludes that the barbershop is "a racial and cultural distinction" from the university campus, the site where we both trained as intellectuals and currently work as professors (2004, 80). Because we participate in both sites, we suffer from the conflict that exists between them. So in order to get along on the (white) campus and in the barbershop, we must alter not the color of our skin but the ways we perform race in each location. These racial performances are most often carried out through language, the way we communicate.

Eversley, for instance, was "uneasy in her barber's chair" as "she listened to the men . . . discussing their plans to [participate in and] make a political statement" during the Million Man March. In what she terms "her best graduate-student speak," she expressed her belief that the march perpetuated the oppression of black women and gays. "For a few seconds, the men . . . seemed to listen," she writes, "[but] then continued with their conversation." Prompted by her barber to persist (he whispered: "Try it again, college girl"), "she offered a picture of her thoughts" (she wrote about herself in the third person for reasons that I explain in note 5). She explained that the "sexism and homophobia" of the march "mirrored the logic of white supremacy." As she left, the men told her she was "still 100 percent black." As she made her way to campus, however, she says she "felt triumphant and sad"—triumphant because, although the men "had read the education in her language as proof of her 'imitation whiteness,'" she was able "to shed her academic self-consciousness" and belong, to be seen as "part of the group, as authentic." She was sad because, "when she arrived on campus," her performance of black authenticity lost its cachet; she realized that the benefits she garnered in the shop were now distinct disadvantages (2004, 80).

Why did Eversley feel split in two? Had she become the twenty-first-century incarnation of Du Bois's double consciousness, an embodiment of racial schizophrenia? One moment she spoke as an "imitation white woman," and after a switch of the tongue, she became an authentically black one. What endowed the barbers with the authority to make her feel race-fake and then authentic? Did her linguistic performance really have such transformative power? Whatever the answers to these questions are, it's clear that Eversley was compelled to contend with the consequence of her performance: the transformation of her political commitments into identity ambivalence.[5]

This racial ambivalence is what makes me so self-conscious about and analytical of other men in the barbershop—because my linguistic performance is rated in relation to theirs. And not only do I feel as if my racial performance is judged, but I know my gender performance is too. Because the barbershop is a masculine space, the performance of heterosexuality is the gold standard. Talking sufficiently black is not enough for me to be heard; I must also speak and act acceptably masculine. This performance is even more difficult for those who are gay or are taken as gay, as I sometimes am, because we are often estranged in these spaces. Quincy Mills (2004) offers Eric as an example in this regard in his ethnography of a black barbershop on the South Side of Chicago.[6]

Mills describes Eric as "one of the regulars in the shop." But unlike other patrons, "his identity is shrouded in suspicion and innuendo," because "the barbers and many customers assume that Eric is gay." As a result, unlike other regulars who become key players in the discourse community, Mills writes that Eric "is silenced as an agenda setter. . . . When [he] would initiate conversations, the men would turn away, ignore him, or patronize him for a short while only to move quickly to other topics." Instead of engaging Eric, they would "act annoyed by his mannerisms and voice" (2004, 187–88).

Mills doesn't describe the particulars of Eric's voice and manner, but it's conclusive that for the others his masculine performance is insufficiently heterosexual. What's interesting about the other men's perception of Eric's sexuality is that it's not based on facts but on how he acts. On this Mills is clear: "Eric never came out to me" or to the other men, he says. "There was no confirmation of his sexual identity in the months I spent at the shop." Eric's insufficient heterosexual performance cast him "outside the boundaries of blackness because his demeanor and speech," Mills writes, "are beyond the narrow definitions of masculinity" (2004, 187–88).

My personal history is replete with anecdotes like Eversley's and experiences like Eric's, and I'm trying to keep them from adding up, which is why I keep my mouth closed in the barbershop. It's also why I was nervous about reading the novel I brought with me to help pass the wait. It's not that novel reading itself is off-limits in the shop. I've seen other men read. But given my past, my profession, and my dubious masculine performance, I hesitate.

Literacy habits, like reading novels of a certain kind and speaking what might appear to be standard English, have always made me seem more queer, more white identified, and more middle class than I am. When I fail to meet the class, gender, and racial notions that others ascribe to me, I'm punished. In some ways, living in a mostly white town and being an assistant professor at a Big Ten school heightens—not lessens, as I had hoped—the conflict that stems from the sometimes converging, but oftentimes diverging, racial and gender expectations that are held out for black men and that we hold for each other.

I recognize the problem, and I'm working so that it doesn't consume me. "Hell," I say to encourage myself, "I'm an English professor; that justifies my reading a novel in a barbershop. And what's this nonsense of trying to fit in, to avoid alienation, to avoid name-calling: 'Sissy!' 'Faggot!'" But I wonder: What does not fitting in cost me? This issue of trying to fit in but never succeeding, of being perpetually on the margins of various communities and never finding a way into any one of them, is the trope of my life, making me something of a black Sisyphus. Academic literacy is my heavy rock.

You see, my Sisyphean experience in Iowa is a continuation of troubles that began while I was growing up in Chicago, in the late 1970s and '80s, in the notorious Governor Henry Horner Homes, the same site that Alex Kotlowitz writes about in his journalistic ethnography, *There Are No Children Here*. In fact, as Kotlowitz was gathering material for his book, I was still living there. But unlike his subjects, Lafeyette and Pharoah, who are portrayed as boys who must fight the criminalizing lure of the ghetto in order to succeed in school, I was seen as an anomaly. Kotlowitz sees Lafeyette and Pharoah as having identities compatible with the ghetto even as he describes their striving to get out.[7] My identity, however, was atypical, alienating me from my neighbors and hood and excluding me from representations of "authentic" ghetto life. Thus I didn't have to fight to get out of the ghetto. I was kicked out.

It might seem like a good thing that I was kicked out. It might seem as if this exile expedited the leave I was seeking. But the problem that this bit of personal history presents, the problem that my monograph theorizes, the problem that my trip to the barbershop illustrates is this: because I ain't no homeboy—though I long to be and would do anything short of killing to gain that identity—I'm not ghetto enough for the ghetto. Because I'm not a white boy, I'm not white enough for white folks. And because I wasn't born into the middle class, I'm not completely accepted by the mainstream. And sometimes, if you can believe it, I'm not ghetto enough for the mainstream or middle class enough for the ghetto or black enough for white folks![8] The psychoemotional pain that this liminal existence creates, the pain of negotiating multiple cultural and racial worlds, is far too great for many. I've been doing it for a long time and have been able to cope only by transforming my personal problem into an intellectual one. In some ways I'm chipping away at the burden. But far too many are not able to do this. And why should they have to?

Perhaps some black men in that barbershop are also trying to avoid racial and cultural punishment. Instead of negotiating two worlds, maybe they have chosen to live in only one—a microcosm, a subculture of white society that accepts and mandates a certain sociolinguistic performance of masculinity. Because they have chosen and are accepted by a community, perhaps they have no need to envy me as I do them. But then what do they lose when they don't try to imitate what I represent? It's my desire to reconcile my ghetto past with my middle-class aspirations and possibly be of assistance to others in the process. I want to expose the factors that make black racial identity incompatible with literacy, especially for males. Thus masculine panic, racial anxiety, and their relation to language and academic literacy (as the prescribed means for class climbing) constitute the three-part theme that I explore in this book.

Introduction

THE BURDEN OF
RACIAL
PERFORMANCE

I'm a dark-skinned black man who spent a good deal of his youth wishing he were white because he believed he was failing miserably at being black. To be sure, I put forth my best efforts to be black, to adjust my speech and behaviors so that they cohered with my race. But the more I tried to acquire an authentic racial identity, the more my efforts revealed my inadequacy. I was just no damn good at it. Trying to be white didn't yield any better results, although, admittedly, I (and others) perceived myself to be closer to what a white boy might be than what I believed a black boy to be. And, speaking honestly, though my desire to be white may not be as intense or as incessant as it was when I was a boy, while it may have dulled significantly, it's still present.

Writing these words is not easy, and it takes all I've got not to keep them private. For I realize that many who know me, who think I'm crazy when I broach this topic, will read this public confession as ultimate evidence that I'm unhinged. Many who don't know me will probably ask: What black man in his right mind would announce, even if it is true, that he wants to be a race other than the one God gave him, especially after the civil rights movement and its follow-up black pride and power movements? Some will recall James Brown's famous lyrics "Say it loud / I'm black and I'm proud" and wonder how I don't get it. Others will hold up my words as evidence of self-hatred, as a sign that my mind has been racially colonized, that white supremacy sits in my consciousness where the slogan "Black Is Beautiful" should be. If I have sympathizers, they might hope for my racial recuperation, doing so with the recognition that it doesn't look good. To admit that on occasion I still wish I were white indicates to some that I'm too far gone.

There is certainly an undeniable element of madness in all this, a psychological aspect to my desires that I don't entirely understand and have yet to fully explore. Even so, that others might consider my words peculiar isn't enough to prevent me from writing these intimate thoughts. It's enough to stall me and, in fact, has in the past. But it's not enough to stop me. After all, sharing is healing. I should say, though, that the healing I'm after is best characterized not by a psychologist but by a linguist—Mary Rhodes Hoover, who, when discussing the resistance of some parents to efforts to teach Black English Vernacular (hereafter BEV) in schools, says their opposition was "not evidence of self-hatred" (1978, 65).[1] In other words, the parents didn't loathe themselves because they didn't want black children to be instructed in the speech that, rightly or wrongly, is considered characteristic of who we are as a people. In order to understand their feelings as something other than self-hate, Hoover recommends a shift in analysis: "The proper interpretation [of their reactions]," she writes, "is sociolinguistic rather than psychiatric" (65).

My reason for offering this tidbit from Hoover is to show how my opening confession, which may not appear at first to be about education, is indeed about language and literacy, especially given that academic verbal skills were the primary means I exploited to perform race not only in school but also in the black community in which I was raised. Hoover's words also verify that my desire to be white does not necessarily mean I hate being black. What it does mean is that whatever factors compel me to prove my blackness and consequently to try to be white are inextricably linked to my life in the hood and my life in school. Thus to comprehend what prompts my racial-cum-linguistic performance in one site depends upon an examination of my performance in the other. This juxtaposition of hood and school forms an analytic lens that Hoover also suggests is appropriate. "In order to properly interpret Black attitudes toward Black English," she writes, "one has to consider schools in relation to settings outside them" (1978, 65–66). And since school and the hood remain racialized as white and black and I remain intimately connected to both, I still perform race in both sites. In fact, as I shall argue, I am required to perform my academic (read white) and ghetto (read black) languages in order to quell and fulfill the racial, class, and gender fantasies that others have of me and that I have of myself.

Hence I'd like to add performance to the sociolinguistic approach that Hoover deems necessary to comprehend black people's perceptions of language and racial identity. I take my cue from the racial performance critic E. Patrick Johnson, who suggests that viewing blackness as a rhetorical performance allows critics to analyze the impact of language and culture upon the various enactments of black identity.[2] This is so, according to Johnson, because performance is "the trope . . . that facilitates the appropriation of blackness" (2003, 6) and, the appropriation of whiteness, as my personal history reveals. Combining Hoover and Johnson, I'd like to call my framework for this project "the sociolinguistics of racial performance" because it suggests the simultaneous study and staging of racialized language habits in social contexts.[3] I use this performance analysis to enact and unpack the details of my racial complex.

It's true I'm writing about my own racial performance, but it certainly isn't true that what I'm writing concerns only me. Nor is it true that the requirement to perform race, to talk white or act black, is only a consequence of my idiosyncratic experience. The fact is, while racial performances may vary among blacks—for example, not everyone wants to be white—the requirement to perform race is pervasive. It's a complex problem that needs to be addressed, particularly where black males and literacy are concerned, as a news article from the *Chicago Sun-Times* highlights.

"Boys Can't Write" (Beaupre 2003) reports that while both black boys and white boys fall behind their female counterparts in literacy skills, black boys are significantly less literate than everyone. Judith Kleinfeld, a psychology professor quoted in the article, suggests that black boys fail because they worry too much about blackness and masculinity and are insufficiently preoccupied with learning to read, write, and speak. According to Kleinfeld, "black guys tend to form a peer group that says, 'School is white, school is sissy.'" Instead of embracing the racial and gender expectations they associate with school, which seem to contradict their self-concept, "they act cool," she says (Beaupre 2003).[4] In short, black males seem to fare worse because they resist most the performances of race and gender that schools appear to demand.

But it's not just black boys who are concerned with how language and school literacy affect perceptions of their racial performance; some black male professors are too. The literacy scholar David Holmes writes, for instance, that while he wishes "to afford African American students more flexibility in constructing their own racialized ethos in writing," an effort he hopes will help them be more successful in school, he admits he desires the same linguistic freedom for himself. The "ulterior motive" behind his research, he reports, arises from "the number of whites and blacks who have told [him] that [his] voice is either 'too black' or 'not black enough'" (2004, ix).

Holmes's bit of personal disclosure shows that it's not just blacks who police other blacks' language habits; whites also impose performance expectations upon us, judging whether we're talking and acting less black than we should or more than what's acceptable and even assessing if we're being too white or not white enough. Thus the formation of school-resistant peer groups among black boys is not an unprovoked outcome of black culture. Rather, these peer groups are responding to the larger cultural phenomenon of equating race with language—a phenomenon that takes the form of imposing, and, as a result, embracing or resisting, racial identity standards.

Similarly, the literacy scholar Kermit Campbell draws attention to the way "over-simplistic characterizations" of language habits as either strictly vernacular or correctly academic have caused his students to question whether they could learn academic language; these characterizations also have caused him to wonder whether, as he says, "I can unequivocally call [academic language] mine in the first place" (1994, 471). Campbell believes, as I will later argue, that it's teachers, not *students,* who create a decisive division between BEV and academic language. He suggests that when teachers operate from an assumption that the two codes are mutually unintelligible, they promote academic failure rather than success. Thus he encourages allowing students and black teachers to combine the two. His iteration of personal concern, however, shows that the goal of such a project remains delayed.

The cultural critic Phillip Brian Harper also reveals a cross-racial linguistic conflict—one he connects to black male gender roles and sexuality. He writes that his "own [linguistic] performance . . . sets [him] up to be targeted as too white-identified or too effete (or both) to be a 'real' black man in certain contexts. That I already identify *myself* as gay," he continues, "may mitigate my vulnerability on that score somewhat" (1996, 205). Harper's case illustrates that language is seen as a means to perform race and is at the same time understood as a performance of gender and sexuality. These dimensions are, like class, so tied to race that whenever racial identity is called into question, they're also invoked, challenged.

Harper's example also hints at why some boys reject literacy when he implies that his "white-identified" blackness and homosexuality are less susceptible to attack in academic contexts. His racial and sexual characteristics are not less vulnerable because academic contexts are more egalitarian, more accepting of difference, but because his characteristics likely fit, although not entirely, the performances that schools require in order for black males to succeed. Consequently, if schools insist that black males behave in ways that are considered, from a cultural perspective, unmasculine or more closely aligned with the ways of white folks, then black males who reject their "white-identified," "effeminate," or "homosexual" counterparts may be acting out their own feelings of rejection by schools. Harper's statement doesn't legitimate this retaliation, but it certainly exposes how school-sanctioned literacy pits groups of black boys against one another. His comment also emphasizes that the problems that both schoolboys and boys in the hood experience are consequences of, as he puts it, "the embattled position that blacks still occupy in this country" (1996, 205).

In view of all this, the concerns of the black boys referred to in the *Sun-Times* article can no longer be dismissed as merely pathological, as the result of their own faulty racial thinking. It can't be said simply that they wrongly desire to be black and masculine rather than literate and have thus created a crisis for themselves. Linking their concerns to my own and to those of the black male professors whom I've mentioned here, I make two interconnected arguments in this book, one about race, the other about language, that will answer why the problem I describe persists for blacks in general and lingers for some despite our educational success.

I contend, first, that exaggerating the differences between black and white languages leaves some black speakers, especially those from the ghetto, at an impasse: either we have to give up our customary ways of speaking and behaving to achieve a measure of mainstream success, risking alienation from family and peers, or we risk remaining in the ghetto. Second, in a similar way, exaggerating and reifying the differences between the races leaves blacks in the impossible position of either having to try to be white or forever struggling to prove we're black enough, which is also configured for males as a struggle to prove we're man enough. Any attempt to meet either choice adds to what I call the burden of racial performance, a burden, I argue, that is always imposed on (and often eagerly accepted by) blacks in ways that it could neither be imposed on nor accepted by whites.[5] Whites don't bear this burden because their primary role is to impose it but also, and perhaps more important, because it is a modern version of what used to be called the "Negro problem." It's a problem formerly defined by this question: What should be done with the Negro? Although the problem remains, the question has changed. It's no longer a question of what should be done with the race but who comprises it: Who belongs to the race?

In James Weldon Johnson's *The Autobiography of an Ex-Colored Man,* a novel that I discuss in chapter 2, there's no doubt about who makes up the race, at least not for the black doctor who tells the nameless protagonist that "we are the race and the race ought to be judged by us, not by them." Johnson's doctor believes that it's the middle-class blacks, not the lower-class blacks he calls "loafing, good-for-nothing darkies," who define the race (1995, 73). His point is clear, though it wasn't exactly true. If you were black in America in the early part of the twentieth century, you were subject to Jim Crow—and in that sense all blacks were the same, sharing the burden of legal discrimination. From the end of Jim Crow till now, however, the doctor's claim has become increasingly important as the burden shifts from color to character. In other words, whether or not you're black becomes more irrelevant as performing the kind of black person you are becomes more crucial.

Because language is often the touchstone for racial performance and consequently for being placed on the imposed identity spectrum, many well-meaning literacy educators who do not wish to impose the burden of racial performance when teaching literacy to black students have offered code switching as a solution. Code switching is a popular concept and approach to language instruction because it appears to be egalitarian. It's supposed to allow students to keep intact their authentic black identity since they are encouraged to speak one dialect and hold one set of beliefs appropriate for the hood (where their dialect and identity are validated) and speak another version of English and adopt thoughts more suitable for school (where they are asked to give up their dialect and identity for a short time in order to achieve the most good in the long run). This is what I embraced and was rewarded for, even though I never quite mastered it. And it's what many of my peers resisted and were punished for. But I don't blame them. Code switching is racially biased, requiring blacks to separate the codes that bespeak their identities from those they use at school. It also breeds linguistic confusion and is as arduous a feat as ever there was one—one that can't be called education but could be seen as an effect of de facto segregation.

True linguistic and identity integration would mean allowing students to do what I call code meshing based on what linguists have called code mixing, to combine dialects, styles, and registers. This technique meshes versions of English together in a way that's more in line with how people actually speak and write anyway. However, although it is more useful than other strategies, code meshing is no panacea. For one, it obscures issues of gender and sexuality by subordinating them to race. And even if that playing field were leveled, like other strategies for teaching literacy, code meshing is not an absolute solution to an abiding racial crisis facing black students. This is not to say that code meshing has no potential to help increase literacy rates and in turn retention rates. I believe it is crucial, if beneficial, for no other reason than that it allows black students (and some teachers) from the ghetto a place in school, a site where many feel alienated. On this basis I argue for code meshing to replace those other linguistic assumptions and ideologies so that the retention rates of black students (and faculty members, for that matter) can improve.

I substantiate my arguments by analyzing some of my own experiences in the sites around which this manuscript is organized: (1) the ghetto, (2) my living room, (3) my brother's house, (4) the classroom, (5) a teachers' meeting, and (6) my university job interview. I have arranged these six sites into two sections, Home and School. Part 1, Home, focuses on how performing race and masculinity impacts and is in turn affected by language and literacy. In School, part 2, I move from my personal life to my professional one, to performing literacy at the college level, with issues related to masculinity and race undergirding that discussion. My discussion of literacy in both parts centers primarily on how the term is used to signify the sanctioned means for class climbing, for elevating someone from ghetto to middle-class status. Viewing literacy in this way, as the trope for black class ascension, allows me to consider the conflicts involved in literacy learning within the larger question of racial authenticity.

Following the advice of the influential linguist Dell Hymes, who writes that "the key to understanding language in context is to start, not with language, but with context" (1972, xix), I portray the ghetto as a matrix of lived experience in chapter 1, "Going Home." Specifically, I describe the Governor Henry Horner Homes housing projects in Chicago where I grew up as the context in which my linguistic habits and concepts of racial identity were first developed. In this personal narrative I illustrate why it is often believed that the ghetto is incompatible with schooling and why intellectual activity is considered a middle-class enterprise. I also depict how these beliefs impact not only me but others from the hood.

In chapter 2, "So Black I'm Blue," I focus on two early twentieth-century passing novels, James Weldon Johnson's *The Autobiography of an Ex-Colored Man* and Nella Larsen's *Passing*—texts that I argue both prefigure and predict the current racial and class tensions between middle- and lower-income blacks. In the context of a family gathering at which I perform an original poem, I argue that the burden of racial performance has supplanted the Jim Crow version of racial passing. The requirement to perform race not only makes it possible for dark-skinned blacks to "pass" but makes it mandatory in order for us to elevate our class status.

In "Nigga-Gender," chapter 3, I discuss why the gender epithet *faggot* is associated with school and why, consequently, the black masculine descriptor *nigga* is associated with the hood. I discuss not only how these terms are used to refer to masculine performances, gender behavior thought to represent sexual practice, but also how they are tied to intra- and interracial class conflicts. This discussion takes place within the context of a visit to my brother's house, where I ponder his avowed nigga status and my ascribed status as a faggot. I explain what these descriptors mean both within the larger societal context and, perhaps most important, for our personal relationship.

In "Your Average Nigga," chapter 4, I recount how I negotiated my own black ghetto-to-middle-class identity conflict as I facilitated classroom interactions with a black male student from the ghetto. I locate the tensions I experienced within the dynamics of race, class, and gender. I argue that it's only when the language of black students/writers is racialized by readers/teachers that their writing and speech are considered nonacademic. I also make an argument against code-switching ideologies as I analyze the positions of other educators, particularly those of other black males.

Sustaining my critique of black teachers who promote code switching, in chapter 5, "Casualties of Literacy," I continue to argue against code switching while discussing what transpired during a teachers' meeting where the mostly white teachers supported a black female teacher who was arguing for it. I claim that black, white, and nonblack liberal educators actually broaden the educational gap between whites and blacks when they support code switching and therefore unwittingly contribute to academic failure among underclass blacks.

In chapter 6, "To Be a Problem," I cycle back to the problems I continue to experience personally as a result of exaggerated notions of race and language. The specific site of focus is my job interview for the professorship I hold at the University of Iowa. I show how that interview was racially marked and how, although I may speak an acceptable version of academic English, there is still a fear among my white colleagues that I may be too black in school.

Narrative performance is central to my analysis in all these chapters. In effect, my arguments arise from my integration of "staging" episodes from my life and "studying" them, making my merger of what's often considered academic (and white) with what's considered creative (and raced) itself a performance of my argument.[6] By performing my argument in this way, by code meshing, I am deliberately shattering the decorum of the scholarly monograph in much the same way that I shatter notions of what it means to be a black man, even as I seek to maintain it (an academic study) and them (traditional notions of race and masculinity). This writing tension mirrors the everyday tension I live and that many blacks live and that materializes into low literacy rates for many, academic success for a few, low school retention rates for most, and wanting to be white and sometimes more black for me.

I am preceded in my efforts by—and indebted to—others who have also used performative writing to expose the tension that education and academic literacy produces for people of color, particularly males. In *Appropriating Blackness* E. Patrick Johnson investigates the connection of racial performance to what he sees as "the arbitrariness and politics of [racial] authenticity [that exist] in language use" (2003, 5). As I do here, he "mark[s] the ways that [he is] implicated in the performance of blackness." Thus, as he studies and writes about others, he also examines the multiple identities he performs as a "black, middle class, southern, gay, male, professor" (10). His text exemplifies what I call the "staging and study" of language and race. But whereas Johnson engages the study of "identity and cultural performance by examining six highly different examples of racial performance" (2), my six examples are connected by a specific focus on how education and literacy intersect with racial performance.

More specifically for me, it's not racial performance itself that is of primary concern in my analysis but the consequences that result when blacks promote or resist the unyielding, unshakeable burden that I argue always accompanies and compromises that performance. And whereas E. Patrick Johnson believes that "the wonderful thing about performance . . . is the space it provides for possibilities and transgressions" (2003, 74), I am not encouraging performance for its subversive potential or otherwise as a way out of essentialized notions of race, gender, and sexuality. In actual fact, I'm echoing the thought that racial performance reinscribes the essentialism it's believed to subvert. I therefore offer another critique of racial performance, an acknowledgment of its limits, an exposé of its failure. Really, some of us—namely, me—are just plain tired of being required to perform all the time.

I also follow the examples set by Keith Gilyard and Victor Villanueva in using racial narrative as the vehicle for making conceptual arguments about language learning. Yet my writing veers from their examples in significant ways. For instance, in his sociolinguistic self-study, *Voices of the Self,* Gilyard separates his analysis from his autobiographical narratives, placing them in alternating chapters, whereas I attempt a seamless combination of the two. Villanueva uses a multivocal approach to compose *Bootstraps.* As he narrates his life story, he shifts from the first to the third person. While this technique is useful to show how individuals embody conflicting identities, I use a conventional first-person narrator, one that I believe is essential to the black autobiographical subject.

Because my interests and commitments in this book are more intellectual and less disciplinary, not solely positioned in performance studies or literacy studies, I'm also influenced by writers and texts that bend toward literary and social criticism. As a result, the two models— one contemporary, the other historical—that have most inspired my project are Michael Awkward's *Scenes of Instruction* and W. E. B. Du Bois's *The Souls of Black Folk.* Awkward, who theorizes how education "placed [him] at odds with social constructions of black maleness," calls his text an "autocritography." Awkward defines this genre as "a self-reflexive, self-consciously academic act" that gives an "account of individual, social, and institutional conditions that help to produce a scholar" (1999, 7).

Autocritography is also a genre, according to Kimberly W. Benston, that integrates personal experience into "texts also devoted to interpretations of African-American literary and cultural performances." For Benston "these autobiographical reflections" that take place in critical texts by black authors "constitute a performative practice that dramatizes the roles of memory, reading, and translation in the construction of modern African-African subjectivity" (2000, 284). Both Awkward's and Benston's descriptions of autocritography fit my attempts in this monograph. Unlike Awkward, however, I have used "autobiographical recall" not only to write a memoir but also to illustrate the intersection between what I call the burden of racial performance and the problems that I and other blacks face in the ghetto and in school, particularly in college.

And just as Du Bois uses autocritography to explain how race led him to "beat [his white] classmates at examination time, or beat them at a foot-race, or even beat their stringy heads," I discuss how race prompts me to excel and also how it fuels my racial anger. Du Bois is also concerned with how race prompts some to fail. As am I, he is disquieted in *Souls* by the plight of "other black boys" for whom "the strife was not so fiercely sunny," those who could not achieve what he achieved, boys whose "youth," he says, "shrunk into tasteless sycophancy, or into silent hatred of the pale world about them and mocking distrust of everything white; or wasted itself in a bitter cry" (1994, 2). It is in his two narrative chapters, in the stories "Of the Meaning of Progress" and "Of the Coming of John," that we get a glimpse of these other boys—and even a glimpse of the sorry state in which education and race place males who have supposedly "made it."

Furthermore, Du Bois sought in his chapters "to sketch, in vague, uncertain outline, the spiritual world in which [black] Americans live and strive" (1994, v). He succeeded by assembling chapters that present social critique, ethnography, history, and even short fiction. Like Du Bois, I vary the style, structural arrangement, and genre of my six chapters. Of course, I'm not claiming that my writing reflects the narrative craftsmanship, rhetorical dexterity, or intellectual prowess of E. Patrick Johnson, Gilyard, Villanueva, Awkward, or Du Bois. I seek only to build upon the patterns they have set, modifying them for my specific purposes here, and to honor them by stating so.

I am pleased that so much scholarship has amassed around literacy and racial performance. It affords me this opportunity to connect my lived experience to that research and to analyze and critique both. Really, theoretical discussion cannot be put to better use—I think—than for someone to wrap his life in it and disclose just how closely or loosely the cover fits, just how much warmth the blanket provides or how much cold it still lets in. A performance analysis, then, of the relationship between race and literacy from a combined personal and professional perspective is what I offer in the pages that follow.

1

HOME

1
GOING
HOME

Heritage

What is the ghetto to me:
Community action, Momma's care
Black folk dancin', singin' everywhere
Corner preacher, Sistah praisin' joyfully
The ghetto is home, what else could it be?

Concrete jungle. Shots in the street.
"Avoid contact with all you meet!"
Estranged family. Dead playmates.
Is the ghetto home, or a site I hate?

People always go back home when they want to go somewhere new, when they want to chart a new course in life, to take what they were and who they may be and make something new out of them. I'm no different. I went back to my childhood home, back to that segment of the black ghetto that the City of Chicago called the Governor Henry Horner Homes housing projects.

I went back to Horner in memory as much as to the actual site—because that part of the complex I called home doesn't exist anymore. I can't walk into the building that stood at 2029 West Lake Street and into apartment 513 and begin to feel my way around the concrete duplex where I grew up. The place Momma, after returning to college, had warned her children would not be around in fifteen to twenty years. She knew that what she was learning in her urban sociology classes at the time was true. "Old Mayor Daley put a simple plan on the books," she would say. "The niggers must go!" We questioned where, but she just said to mark her word and wait to see if the buildings and we would be gone.

True to her word, they are and we are—though not all of them or all of us. My oldest sister remains, with her two kids and husband. And I have an aunt who lives there with her daughter and six grandkids. This is the daughter whose live-in boyfriend was found dead in the schoolyard of my old elementary school. Some think he was killed in some strange way. "Shot up with some kind of poison," they say; "Overdosed," others believe, "on the crack he liked." Stories like his keep me from going back often. And when I do, I don't ask many questions, so I still don't know whether the boyfriend died of an accidental overdose, was murdered, got juiced with some bad junk, or committed suicide. Henry Horner is the ghetto, and, like any other ghetto, it has secrets I don't want to know and would probably refuse to tell if I did.

But Horner's not like Logan Square, where I lived when I was in graduate school. Logan Square is an "up and coming" neighborhood on the near northwest side of Chicago, where my brother-in-law reconstructed a defunct homeless shelter into six luxury condos. I rented the one that his mother had occupied before she went to live in a senior citizen building. "No quiero estar aqui," she said and kept repeating that she did not want to be there until she had packed everything she wanted to take into a few small bags and was gone by evening. "She wanted to play cards with her friends," my brother-in-law told me.

Logan Square wasn't always a safer neighborhood than the one I came from. It changed after it was gentrified and middle-class whites moved in. The redeveloped buildings on either side of where I lived were occupied mostly by transplanted white suburbanites who kept me up all night with their weekend drinking parties and marijuana smoke that seeped through my windows. I saw their bloodshot eyes on Monday mornings, observed their groggy dispositions and the wrinkled khakis they were wearing to work again, going to good jobs. The biggest pothead was the one professional who actually wore expensive suits and well-coordinated ties and who lived in the condo above mine. We never talked, never so much as waved. But I knew from my brother-in-law that the tall, sandy blond, well-built man with a little leftover baby fat was in his twenties like me and worked downtown. He was one of the reasons I felt safe there. For I believed that if the police came to protect anyone in my building, they'd come because most of the inhabitants were of his race, not mine.

I observed the demeanor of the police during their occasional visits to my block. Their eager, interested expressions made them appear more concerned about my neighbors than I remember officers' being about residents in the ghetto, even children, children like those I saw playing on the concrete playground during my return visit to Horner. Those children danced in my mind until I was able to sigh out of sadness and exhaustion in my condo. It's a tiring task to think back on the past, to let all you've stowed away come flying forward. So to relax I ran some bathwater and lit the candles. My Nina Simone CD played in the background, just above a hum. I chuckled, feeling self-conscious and a little self-righteous, knowing that some of my childhood friends from Horner would probably say this scene sealed it; they'd call me a sell-out, a wannabe, a white boy, a faggot. I tried to allow the lavish amenities of my apartment to assuage the memories, to vindicate me in the face of such insults. But just as they used to, the taunts came barreling forth, landing on my heart with a thud. The anxiety lingered as I soaked in my oversized tub with the six-jet Jacuzzi and replayed the visit in my head.

It's one of those not-rare-enough occasions when I return to Horner to confront all that I was and hope I'm not anymore, all that I hate but fight to love. I'm performing race, as I always am when I go back, donning the appropriate getup for the occasion. Sometimes I'm the loving uncle, casually decked out in khaki pants and a light blue shirt, K-Swiss sneakers, or brown Oxford shoes—my favorite white boy outfit. When I wear this ensemble, I'm ready to show my niece and nephew the world beyond the eight-block radius they call life, encouraging them not to tattoo their bodies and to stop wearing those hip-hop pants that hang halfway down the ass and those skin-tight dresses that make the booty poke out. But then I take them to some swank restaurant downtown, and the manager is a white girl with hair dyed a color none of us can name, with piercings through her eyelids, ears, and lips, indicating they may also be in places we shouldn't know about. My niece and nephew look at her, then at me. "Did you see her, Uncle?" they ask. "Yes," I say quickly, hoping they don't also ask, "Why must we change?" I'm still trying to figure out an answer for them—and myself—for why she's not forced to shape up, knowing full well that if we were in her place, we'd have already been shipped out.

Other times when I go back I'm careful to wear jeans and a sweatshirt. That's when I'm the see-I'm-not-better-than-you cousin and nephew coming to some party that my cousin is throwing for one of her kids or coming to eat because my aunt has fried catfish, barbecued some ribs, or cooked collard greens and invited me. I pull out my spare pair of nearly two-hundred-dollar Nikes, which I keep clean and ready for such times. I don't want to stand out too much. Looking like someone interested in sports is important here.

On this visit, however, I'm suited up: tie, jacket, leather briefcase. I'm a Bible-toting Christian, a Jehovah's Witness. Jeffrey, a friend of mine from the congregation, is with me. We're making an informal call on a man who is studying the Bible. The previous Saturday I'd left my Bible in the car, and Marvin, the man we're calling on, had lent me one of his. In addition to wanting to give back his Bible, I'm intrigued by Marvin. He's in his late forties, perhaps early fifties, dark-skinned with glasses and a slightly cocked-eye that unsettles me. It seems as if he's looking straight through me. I managed to avoid looking in his eye for the first half-hour or so of the Bible study last week, until he started saying, "Hey, you" to get my attention. I finally said, "It's Vershawn; My name's *Ver*shawn." And unlike others who call me every variation of Rashod or Vashon, he remembered it like nothing. "Oh, Vershawn," he said, making sure to pronounce the *Ver* just as I had.

Marvin lives in one of the seven or eight Henry Horner Homes buildings still left to be redeveloped. They're a remnant of my mother's prophecy, of what once was and probably shouldn't have ever been. I park my brand new Toyota in the lot across the street, undisturbed by a sign that says all unauthorized vehicles will be towed. I know the sign is a hollow warning, like most rules here that outsiders must enforce.

The security officer on duty in the building is someone Jeffrey knows. They talk about old times in the projects while Jeffrey mixes in snippets about the Bible. I look around, trying to avoid being conspicuous. I don't want to see anyone I know or knew. I don't want that kind of conversation today. I don't want any of my childhood schoolmates, especially not the ones who used to tease me, to now say, as they always do: "I'm so proud of you. We knew you'd be something. You were always smart." And although they probably won't say it to my face anymore, I don't want any of them to call me queer names behind my back.

I don't want to think about how academically competitive they were in elementary school. How skilled they were in science and math, the arts, and sports. I don't want to get a headache from wondering whether they could just as easily be professors—or doing something even better. I want to be intellectual in my remembering—objective— as I turn a pseudoethnographic lens on my childhood community. To achieve objectivity I'll have to suppress the silent laughter that shows in my eyes—the look I use to tease the former classmates who used to call me faggot. I'll have to conceal the mocking smirk that I know they see but ignore when I silently ask: "Who's the sissy boy now? Look at me, I can leave this place. Where can you go?" I try to resist condescension. But it's my only retaliation—my only relation to them now. I try hard not to feel this way, but when I hurt, it's automatic. I don't want to feel sorry for them, as if I'm somehow better. That's why objectivity would be nice, since I wouldn't have to feel at all.

As Jeffrey talks to the security officer, I look across an empty lot and recall the church where my eighth-grade graduation was held. It's been two or three years since it burned down. "Arson," some rumor. "The pastor needed money." But I refuse to believe it. It doesn't matter what I believe, though. That's the way it goes here. No one, not even the ghetto dwellers, believes anything legitimate happens in the black ghetto. Someone's always trying to scheme and get over. And I can't blame them if it's true.

I let my eyes wander to the spot where 2029 used to stand. A redevelopment complex of luxury-looking apartments and townhomes has replaced it. The townhomes were originally intended for people of all income levels and races. But it seems that no one wants to live next door to poor blacks. That part of the old neighborhood is now called the West Haven complex. It stretches westward on the south side of Lake Street, from Damen Avenue to Oakley Street, exactly where the old Horner buildings used to stand. In this section of Horner there were three buildings that were seven stories high and four that were fifteen stories high. We called the entire group of seven the "Reds" or "News." 2029 was one of the seven-story Reds. It stood right at the intersection of Lake Street and Damen Avenue. To get to it we didn't have to go around or through any of the other buildings. And no other building blocked its view from passengers who rode the Lake and Damen buses or the L-train that passed right outside our windows.

The brown buildings that stretch eastward from Damen Avenue to Hermitage Street, the ones that remain, mostly border Washington Boulevard, with a few along Lake Street. These were the original buildings of Horner. They look more like Cabrini Green, the buildings in the opening scenes of *Good Times*, the late 1970s TV show that depicted an all-black family that was coping with daily life in the housing projects of Chicago. We used to call these remaining Horner buildings the "Olds," apparently because they were built first.

The Reds looked different. They weren't fully enclosed like the Olds, where you immediately entered a hallway area when you exited your apartment. Instead the Reds were built with what we called porches or ramps, long concrete slab floors, enclosed by wrought-iron fences that looked like prison gates with a million little holes. Each opening was only big enough for you to ball up a candy wrapper and fit it through so that it fell into a grassless grave. One story goes that the fences on each floor were built only three-quarters of the way up but were raised after a small child climbed over and fell to its death.

Another version has the child being thrown by an angry mother, giving the housing authority no choice but to enclose the place.

Damen Avenue not only divided the Reds from the Olds, but it also separated rival gangs, the Vice Lords from the Black Disciples. The Olds were Vice Lord territory, the Reds were Disciple territory, I think. Though it seemed to be occupied by the Vice Lords, 2029 was neutral territory—probably because of its location. All this is hazy for me because, for one, I didn't have many friends there (nor do I have any informants now). And, two, Momma kept us from knowing such things, kept us from playing downstairs on the playgrounds, from having too many friends, and even from family members, cousins who lived a few blocks away in the Olds, who couldn't even stay overnight.

Our cousins would come to our apartment unannounced—the way family members do sometimes. Momma would tiptoe to the door, look through the peephole, and dare us with her eyes to make a sound. When our cousins were exhausted from knocking, they gave a final hard kick to let us know they knew we were home. Momma would return to doing whatever it was she had been doing, pretending like nothing had happened, as if we hadn't just ignored family. And even before caller ID she'd know by the time of day who was calling and forbade us to answer the phone.

Momma considered herself a good Christian. She constantly quoted 1 Corinthians 15:33, saying, "Bad association spoils useful habits." That included anything outside our home. We even had to be careful about who we talked to at church. She tried to protect us when she'd close the door. She locked the ghetto out. She told us not to get too close to it when it walked the streets or wanted to visit, reeking of alcohol or drugs. She tried to shield us from the violence that seemed to lurk everywhere.

When I was growing up, it seemed that at the oddest times, some of them during periods of peace—respites from the violence when the gangs would come to a truce, sign a peace treaty, or, I suppose, would just get tired—there would be a killing. Once, a man, a gang leader, died right outside my aunt's apartment door. And on more than one occasion a stray bullet shattered one of our fifth-floor apartment windows and lodged in one of the concrete walls. Fortunately, no bullet ever lodged in one of Momma's sons' eyes. That happened to a boy I went to school with. He lived on the first floor in one of the Olds, not far from me. He was simply playing in the kitchen. All the news channels covered the story.

Later that year, once the boy was well, a news station did a special story on the accident. The reporter said the boy was lucky to be alive, that the effects of gang violence often end more tragically. What she implied was that at times a bullet found rest in some kid's heart and the residents would hope the dying child wasn't the younger sister or daughter of one of the gang members. If so, there'd be war for days.

One time the Black Disciples came into the Vice Lord territory as I walked northward along Damen Avenue, from Madison Street, returning home from the currency exchange where Momma had sent me to buy postage stamps. They asked me: "Wha' chu ride?" and "What's yo' sign?" They wanted me to identify my gang affiliation and to demonstrate the hand signals used to represent it. When I couldn't, some of the boys told the leader, "He ain't no hook, man. He ain't no hook." The leader demanded money anyway, so I gave him Momma's 28 cents in change. He then hit me on the forehead with his fist, in which was enclosed the barrel of his gun.

Another time our apartment door was burned. The story we heard was that the Black Disciples didn't know exactly which of two apartments belonged to the family of one of the Vice Lords. So they burned both doors with homemade bombs, some kind of cocktail they called it, made with a rag stuck in a glass pop bottle filled with gasoline. We knew the family they wanted lived next door in 514, and the son was in jail at the time. But that's the way it happened here.

People got desensitized to the violence. Kids played freely on the playground and forgot all about gangs. After all, a brother, cousin, friend, or someone they knew and loved was probably in a gang and promised protection. In the midst of their playing there'd be a gun shot. All would run quickly into the nearest apartment. But you had to close your door fast or a gang member might try to hide there too. Others were thrill seekers or had been assigned as lookouts and sought cover only in one of the building hallways, where they could sneak a peek. The shooting would last only a moment sometimes. Other times it would be five minutes, no longer than ten, I think. Then someone would give the all-clear sign, and everyone would go back outside. The kids would swing on the swings, climb the monkey bars, and play in the sandbox, being careful not to cut themselves on broken glass.

We never went out after a shooting. Momma kept all eight of us indoors, which wasn't easy. My three older brothers wanted to go out and play sports with the other boys and flirt with girls. I wanted to meet and play with my friends. And my four older sisters longed to play double-dutch on the porch. They also found it hard sometimes not to be flattered by the boys who lingered for hours outside our door. But Momma was determined not to have boys who were in gangs or teenage girls who'd make her a grandmother. When people ask me how she did it, how we made it, I tell them I'm not sure; that's Momma's story to tell. What I remember besides her bluffin', cussin', and prayin' is that she would say there was more to life than Horner and required only that we get out and find it.

Remembering the violence prevents me from coming to Horner as often as I might and motivates me to make my infrequent returns short. But I'm with Jeffrey, and he's naturally slow, with no concept of time. He says he's never cared about time—"Africans don't care about that," he told me once, "we're a rhythm people. We move with the flow." I look over to where he's standing, still talking to the officer, and shoot him my best "Let's go, slow poke" frown. My intrigue is giving way to angst, and I just want to give Marvin his Bible back and go.

I'm getting more and more tired of trying to ignore the broken elevator, though I'm secretly thankful when it doesn't work. The floor would probably have puddles of piss, and we'd wind up walking upstairs anyway. Even though I make most of these visits in the daytime, the stairways are dark, the lights are busted, and then I'm scared. And once I get to the floor I'm going to, the walls are filled with graffiti, and I find myself reading that someone's mother is a "dick sucking dyke" and her kids are "bitches" or that the "Four Corner Hustlers still rule" or that the "Vice Lords are king." I know that the graffitists probably don't even live here, and the residents have either stopped trying to care or don't have enough energy left to fight.

I'm happy I don't live here. When I did, I couldn't stand the dirt, the filth, the smeared, dried feces on the wall, and the Pine Sol smell of the mildewed mop that the maintenance worker used to try to clean. But these buildings are impossible to clean, and the apartments carry that same I-can't-get-clean look. "I'm scrubbed; I'm mopped; I really am!" they scream. Then out of sadness and acquiescence, they whisper, "I'm uncleanable."

The state of these buildings was inevitable. Momma used to keep our apartment clean, both the upstairs with its one bathroom, four bedrooms, and two big hallway closets, and the downstairs with a nice-sized foyer right when you walked in and a very large eat-in kitchen and living room. They were really nice apartments, even if they were made of concrete, though we used to say that the housing authority probably would have maintained them better if white folks had lived in them.

When redevelopment was beginning, families were given options—one was to use Section 8, a program that allowed them to move into other neighborhoods on federal grants that subsidized their housing costs by paying the landlord a percentage of the rent. There was also scattered-site housing, one or two small buildings of subsidized housing that were placed in supposedly better neighborhoods throughout the city. We never moved into one of these. Momma said she liked the heat in the Horner apartments and the central location close to downtown. She would say that you could get anywhere in the city from where we lived. It was true. We lived two blocks north of Madison, the city's north-south dividing line, and on every other street or so there was either a bus line or an L-train station.

But we were forced to move out when I was a junior in high school. Momma was paying six hundred dollars for rent—30 percent of her monthly gross income. That wasn't the part that made us move, though. She would have stayed because of the heat, the familiarity, and the location, and because she would still have to pay only 30 percent of whatever she was making if she lost her job. If it were 30 percent of almost nothing, then she'd pay that. She considered that security. But when families who lived in the apartments next door and over and under us all moved, and the housing authority stopped heating those apartments, and gangbangers, bad kids, and strays went into them and turned on the water, the pipes would burst and our apartment would flood. The housing authority came once to sweep the water out of our apartment and that time only because the janitor was a distant cousin of my grandmother's from down South. Our apartment flooded every other day for the two or three winters Momma tried to stick it out.

It's been more than a few minutes, and Jeffery's conversation is finally cut short because the security officer has darted off. I'm shocked and look to where he's headed. He's running alongside a regular cop, and they both are chasing a boy, a teenager with braids, who from the side is a Snoop Doggy Dogg look-alike—and, boy, is he running fast. Jeffrey's friend is running faster than the white cop, who is dressed in the official blue of the Chicago PD and who was obviously chasing the boy first.

I turn around and notice that a white car, an old Chevrolet sedan made into a hoopty, complete with shiny silver rims, extra shock for bounce, and added rear and front bumpers, is in the middle of the street with the driver's side door open. Another boy is in the backseat. That door is open too. He's handcuffed. And there's no apparent explanation. I stand there, surprised at myself for hoping the running officers wouldn't catch the boy. And if they do, I pray: "Please, God, let it be the black cop. And if he has any sense, let him pretend to struggle with the boy and let him go." I pray not only for the boy's escape, knowing the fate of black men who get hefty punishments for petty crimes, but also for the security guard to act with insight and not with a slave's mentality.

His enthusiasm in the chase reminds me of attempts made by some blacks to put themselves at odds with other blacks in order to gain favor from whites. It's like the overzealous slave carrying out the overseer's dirty work—beating other slaves, snitching on them—for a few more measly scraps of fat. I can't fathom that a white security guard, with no police training, no gun, no badge, no authority, would run after a white kid that two black cops are chasing. If a white cop engaged in such a chase, would he not struggle a little with the white boy and then let him go? If the black guard is running after the boy to turn him over to the white cop, then I don't believe he's doing it in the name of "justice for all" but as a way to separate himself from the boys, to show that all blacks are not criminals—putting himself in danger, doing more than the white cops are willing to do, and thus embracing a burden that'll only get heavier as he tries to prove his difference. It's actions like his—if my perception is right—that exacerbates antagonism within the race, that keeps blacks in conflict with other blacks, trying to prove who's better, who's worse, putting whites in the place of God, giving them final say on which blacks are acceptable and which are not.

Jeffrey and I have seen and lived through worse than a small-scale police chase. We're not afraid, since, from the looks of it, no bullets will fly. Yet the scene reminds me of so much I've tried to escape, and I hate that I decided to come this time. I certainly could have waited to give Marvin his Bible back. "What the hell was I thinking?" I ask myself, especially when the mixed pine smell hits me and a woman runs past me to see what's happened. She has no front teeth and looks rundown, with her breasts flopping around inside her loose pink tank top. I could tell she was attractive once, not so long ago probably, before the hardship set in. I didn't want to be too hard on her, thinking how she could be a victim of circumstances. But I wonder how complicit she is with those circumstances. Does she know better? Can she do better? I shake my head, feeling just as complicit in racist thinking as the guard I prayed for. I close my eyes for a moment and pray for myself.

Jeffrey finally says, "We better get up to Marvin's," like he just thought of it and I was the African taking all day. I nod in agreement, and we ride up to the fifth floor, where Marvin lives. Marvin's eye darkens the peephole and, just as I'm about to say my name, Jeffrey catches my attention. He tells me that he likes being with me, that our friendship has endured some ten years because he has allowed me to be myself. He says he doesn't care that I spent so much time in school, something Jehovah's Witnesses discourage. He also says it doesn't bother him that I talk so much about racial politics and other things unrelated to scripture. I recognize the condescension. Although I know his, like mine, comes from a place of insecurity, I can't stop myself from looking him up and down, pausing at his yellow teeth layered with tartar. He has a few small specks on the front two from something he's just finished chewing. He has ring around the collar on his overly wrinkled shirt, and his suit pants are bulky at the waist because he wears sweat pants underneath. His bag is stuffed with items he doesn't need. He stands in stark contrast to me: neat, orderly, and always clean, as I think anyone should be. I utter thanks to God that I am different. But then I wonder: What has difference cost me?

"Who's knocking?" Marvin asks impatiently. I think it's an original way to ask, "Who is it?" Or "Who's at the door?" And that makes me like him even more. Inside, Marvin warns us that something is going on downstairs. I take his announcement as license to go to the window. Three additional police cars have joined the scene. This is curious because it's certainly more than the usual none that I remember showing up in the hood when I was a boy when gangs fought or openly sold drugs. Jeffrey sits and chats with Marvin. I remain standing because what's going on outside is too familiar and I want to leave right away. I'm stuck for the moment, though, because something Jeffrey said has preoccupied me, and I don't want to leave until I've figured it out.

The other part of the left-handed compliment he gave me in the hall, besides his letting me be myself, was that he admired me for going to school, for getting a PhD. He said he always wanted to do what I'm doing, instead of working as a mail clerk in a small office building on the edge of downtown. He intends his words to flatter, and they do—a little. I know, however, that neither he nor I have the handle we need on our insecurity for it not to create conflict between us. He is going to have to prove to me and to himself that what he chose to do is just as good as what I'm doing. I'm used to that now. And I'll let him go on until he gets on my nerves. Then I'll have to take him someplace that he won't have access to or will feel uncomfortable about unless he's with me, like a fancy restaurant in one of the gentrified neighborhoods. That will keep him silent for a day or two, while he also thinks about difference. That's just long enough for me to regroup.

Marvin's apartment is of the cleaner type. He's a handyman in the building, so it fits. The apartment is decorated with pictures of his only daughter, who's away at college, and he has several small bookcases that are filled with recipe books, books about understanding the Bible, and do-it-yourself manuals. He has nice brown furniture with blue trim and a color TV in a console that is placed not too prominently in front of the sofa. It's over to the side a bit so that conversation and books take the focus. It's in just the spot I plan to place mine in my apartment when I can afford a nice big TV.

As Jeffrey talks, I nod in agreement every now and again to give the impression that I'm listening as I continue to stand, glancing out the window, remembering 2029. It was there, mostly within the confines of our apartment, that I grew up. I was surrounded by books on urban issues from my mother's schooling. There were also a bunch of medical books because she had become a registered nurse after earning an associate degree in nursing, before returning to get a bachelor's degree in sociology. She raised her kids as Jehovah's Witnesses, a very literate Christian denomination; reading and speaking are a part of every service. So religion books were around the place too.

Those books and my siblings were my company, since I either feared or hated everything else outside our four walls. School was no exception, even though I liked learning. Many teachers, students, and even the principal disliked me. To them I seemed like an odd little boy, coming to school in the fourth grade with a tie and jacket on, trying to convince the other students that a man can actually turn into a roach if he's not careful, and I had the book to prove it. Momma had to do a report on Kafka's *Metamorphosis,* and I had read through the book, taking the allegorical parts literally. When the teacher sent a note home saying I was too argumentative, Momma tried to explain the book to me, but her explanation made no sense. Besides, I liked mine better.

In the seventh grade I had gotten tired of going to the school district's science fair and not winning, not even getting any one of the ten prizes. So I asked a judge, a black woman who taught at another school, why I never won. I was bright, brighter than most of the white kids who were too quiet and mumbled through their presentations. I was always cheery and did my presentation with pride, inflecting my voice to add drama as I discussed the stages of my experiment. I knew I just had to win. The teacher showed me the score sheet and said I couldn't win because I didn't have a research paper. I was in the seventh grade and had never done a research paper. I was red hot that my school had sent me to the science fair for the third year straight with only an abstract explaining my experiment, which my teacher had written, knowing full well I couldn't win.

I couldn't wait to get back to school to let my teacher have a piece of my mind. I marched straight to my class, and while the other students were reading silently, I whispered to her what the judge had told me. She turned fiery red and said in a very loud voice: "How dare you, Vershawn? As much as I do for you kids. . . . How dare you?" With that statement she sent me to the office. I had no luck convincing the principal that I'd done nothing wrong.

The principal said I had an attitude problem and that she needed to work with me—help me out before I went to high school. She had her best and final chance when she refused to allow me to give the valedictory speech for the eighth-grade graduation. Every student and teacher in the building knew that no student could outshine me. I had won every oratory and science contest since fifth grade. My reading and math scores were always two to three years ahead. She said it was my attitude. She gave the valedictory to a boy who was always on my heels but couldn't keep up, a boy who always won second place in the science fair. She gave the salutatory to a boy who moved into the neighborhood and had transferred to our school that very year. She said they were quiet and were models for our school. "You have a bad attitude," she said. "You can't represent this school."

I think she was trying to teach me not to be too arrogant around white folks, even though she herself was black. I was supposed to affect mock humility, to know my boundaries, and accept the limitations that growing up black would place around me. She also didn't want me to show too much confidence in my abilities around other black folks. They'd think I was trying to be better, trying to be white. I probably should have learned those lessons. But I refused. "Why should I?" I'm sure I thought. "This is the eighties. Jim Crow is over. I have rights." Because of that thinking I found myself in quite a bit of trouble during my school years, including college, and even during those first years of teaching in mostly white high schools.

By sixth grade Momma had introduced us to E. Franklin Frazier's *Black Bourgeoisie*. I devoured what she said and took it to school, trying to convince the teachers that, since Momma was fluctuating between jobs as a social worker and nurse, we were a part of the black middle class. I made one black teacher so angry that she said it was impossible for me to be bourgeois because, first off, the middle class doesn't live in housing projects, and, second, I was too dark. By eighth grade I had read through Harold Cruse's *The Crisis of the Negro Intellectual*. This time I made sure I let that teacher know I didn't want to be bourgeois; they weren't any good. They didn't like us. And I asked her why members of the black bourgeoisie came to teach us ghetto kids, anyway, if we could never be counted among them.

I was sent home and told not to return without my mother. But Momma wasn't going. She had always told her boys—and her girls too—that if we got sick, got hit by car, or somehow or another wound up in the hospital, she would come see us. But if we were ever put in jail or sent home from school, she wasn't going. And she meant it. One of my brothers had to spend the night in jail because he had sneaked out late one night and got picked up for violating curfew. Momma refused to go get him even though the police threatened to take her to jail if she didn't. She was teaching us how to survive, to stay out of jail, as best we could, and to see the importance of education. Obviously, she saw avoidance, the try-your-best-not-to-get-into-trouble strategy, as best.

This was my first time being sent home from school, but Momma still whipped me with an extension cord and reminded me of my place with adults. I went to the school for a week, begging them to let me back in. The principal had to keep me because it was against the law, she said, to send me home alone. So she let me sit in the office and write *I will behave in school*. After a week she and I decided enough was enough. She told me not to come back, and I was determined not to. So I turned in my books to the office, forgetting that I had put a note inside that I had written to another student. We had been planning a surprise birthday party for the teacher. Being sent home had made me mad, however, and I wrote that I wouldn't give her a party if my life depended on it, that I hated her ass. I wrote the note in red ink because it was all I could find.

My grandmother was living with my cousins, who had by now moved from the Olds to the first floor of 2029. On Monday she took me back to school. During the conference the principal said that I'd written the note as a threat. She took the red ink as a symbol of my teacher's blood and suggested I see a psychiatrist.

I laughed uncontrollably, my body shaking hard, my eyes watering. The principal got angry and stopped the meeting and told my grandmother to take me home. She said that I was enjoying the conversation too much, that I wasn't normal. She said that I could come back to school the next day if my grandmother agreed to the psychiatric evaluation. By the weekend the principal had sent a letter recommending the doctor, the evaluation, and a voucher so that the visit would be free. The letter angered Momma. "You got those people thinkin' you crazy. You ain't crazy and you know it."

But by this time I wasn't sure, and I wanted to go just to find out. I told Momma that living in the projects can't be good and that the teachers weren't teaching anything to us ghetto kids, except how to be less than white people. "Don't your urban sociology classes teach you that?" I asked. When she slapped me, I assumed they did and that it was too painful to accept, especially when there was so little she could do about it.

Standing at Marvin's window puts me in something of a trance, so much so that I don't realize at first that the police are leaving Washington Boulevard. I turn around and blurt out, "Jeffrey, I'm ready to go." He looks surprised and feigns hurt. So I play along and soften my tone: "The police are leaving. I think it's a good time to make our move." He agrees. Marvin notices the strained expression on my face and asks me what I'm thinking about. "Those two boys," I say, launching into a story about how being black and male with braided hair and playing rap music would have been enough to cause the arrest of one and the chase after the other. I tell him that things aren't always what they seem. He looks askance after my commentary and smacks his lips—probably because I left out rote references about God's ridding the earth of crime and violence.

I didn't tell him what I thought about the little kids who kept playing jump rope and hopscotch while the whole ordeal with the police was going on. I didn't tell him that the scene with these kids recalls my cousin's boyfriend's fate and is a sign of thick irony for me. It was kids, probably some of the same ones playing, who discovered his body early one morning outside my former elementary school; the bootstraps that many conformists wish he'd used to pull himself up were doubled under him, his breathless back propped against the bricks of the very institution that many would say was designed to save him. The visual paradox of his death epitomizes for me what happens when civil leaders and educators berate and exclude those who most need to be saved.

Like those educators, however, the paradox of his death also feeds my ambivalence. At times I'm committed to improving schooling for those from the ghetto; at other times I lose faith in education; and on occasion I've been known to chastise the black poor for lack of ambition. I feel like a hypocrite sometimes, a failure; other times I feel there's not much I can do, and I ask, "What good is it that I'm a ghetto-boy-turned-college-professor if I couldn't help him or his kids?"

Just weeks before my cousin's boyfriend died, he had called me, the first and last time, to ask that I transfer his boys from the neighborhood school. He said they weren't learning anything and asked if I could enroll them at a better school close by, the one where I was an apprentice principal. But as an intern I didn't have any influence. Plus, I was too vocal about the educational injustices I perceived and, at twenty-six, possibly too young and considered too militant to be taken seriously. I was in constant battle with the official, award-winning, Italian American principal. I didn't even bring his question to her, because I'd watched her turn away parents like him many times before, transferring stigma from father to son, claiming "overcrowding" or that she "couldn't admit kids from another district."

My cousin's boyfriend wanted help navigating the unwieldy Chicago public school system for his kids' sake—a request that pokes holes in the simple narrative many may want to believe: that some deadbeat junkie got the fix of his life and left an unwed mother and six kids to pay for it. But things aren't always what they seem. He was a father who worked everyday to provide for his family, who wanted his kids to receive a good education, and who tried to create the opportunity for them to get one. I wonder now how the principal's prejudice and my unwillingness to speak out against it will increase the negative consequences of his death for his family. I wonder whether the kids who found him think their lot will be like his. I wonder: Do they even care? Or are they learning not to? If so, who's teaching that to them?

I didn't ask Marvin these questions, nor did I say that it makes me sick to look at all those boarded-up buildings in the neighborhood. But I suspect that Marvin connects with me through the silence because he winks and resumes talking to Jeffrey. He knows I'm not telling everything. Anyone who knows me also knows that I take being black seriously, and at times I feel so helpless about it. I didn't discuss these racial politics with Marvin because the Bible discussion is supposed to lighten him. I didn't want to burden him with all that.

I turn and look over my shoulder and take one last peek out the window. One police car is left. The black security guard is talking loudly to the white cops in the car. He seems intent on getting them to see how bad he is for chasing after the boy, whom, thank God, they didn't catch. I see only the one who was handcuffed earlier; now he is lying sideways in the back of the police car in a semifetal position.

As the last police car drives away, Jeffrey and I make our way to the car. I get in and drive fast, looking straight ahead, noticeably irritated. Jeffrey asks me if I'm angry at him for talking too much. He says he always gets excited when he talks about the meaning of Jesus Christ's sacrifice for humanity. He says he can't say he's sorry for talking about that but that he's sorry he dominated the conversation. But he's not stupid. He knows I wasn't listening. What he wants me to tell him, but what I decide to keep to myself, is that I'm irritated at the way the memories came rushing back, mixing remembering with reality. He wants to know my memories—ones I haven't had a chance to figure out.

As I drive, I can't shake the picture of the playing kids, laughing, jumping on hardened patches of glass-glittering dirt, where grass and a few small trees once grew. They're in the middle of a wasteland, where, according to Momma's stories, a thriving community used to be, a community that is now virtually empty, deserted, reminiscent of the end of a bad Western. I drive faster, trying to leave behind the memories. I don't want the dark shadows I'm ashamed of to follow me to my new home. But when I get there, they're with me. So I run some bathwater and light the candles. Nina Simone sings in the background, just above a hum, and I remember . . .

SO BLACK
I'M BLUE

"White people don't know how to tell the difference between one black man and another," writes the comedian Chris Rock in his book *Rock This!* "If they could, we'd all get along" (1997, 11). So Rock declares, "I love black people, but I hate niggers." For he believes that if whites could distinguish good blacks from bad ones, everything would be okay. We'd finally be able to determine which blacks to eliminate because, as Rock says, "the niggers have got to go" (17). Apparently, some whites agree. In Nella Larsen's *Passing,* John Bellew presents an earlier version of Rock's quip when he teases his wife, Clare. "She was as . . . white as a lily," he says. "But I declare she's gettin' darker and darker. I tell her if she don't look out, she'll wake up one these days and find she's turned into a nigger" (1997, 39). Both jokesters get laughs but are duped by the paradox they spin. Bellew learns that his wife really is a nigger. And Rock must answer, What am I?

Rock thus reproduces for himself what I call the burden of racial performance, the demand to prove what type of black person you are. It's a burden all blacks bear, and it is the core of the problem of black racial authenticity. It is the modern variant, I argue, of racial passing, making Bellew's racial distinction archetypal of Rock's performative differentiation.[1] Further, this burden both supports racial discord between whites and blacks and provokes blacks to abhor other blacks, causing Rock to exclaim, "It's like our own personal civil war." This conflict, however, is not only interpersonal, as it is presented in Rock's example: "Every time black people want to have a good time . . . some ignorant ass niggers [are present,] fucking it up. . . . Can't go to the movies first week it opens. Why? Because niggers are shooting at the screen" (1997, 17). It's also intrapersonal as I describe in a crack of my own, in a poem I've titled "shiny."

as dark as i am and tryin' to pass
somebody needs to kick my black ass
for using proper english all the time
when the rest o' my family's spittin' rhyme
dressin' all preppy, talkin' all white,
somebody tell me this ain't right

my skin so black folks think maybe it's blue;
who am i foolin', Two Eyes? Cain't be you
I wash and scrub and cosmetically bleach
but this doggone pigment just won't leach
so tryin' to be white ain't working at all,
since the only attention I get is in the mall
when heads turn to see the nigga with the silver dollar tongue
wondering, who dat talking deep from the diaphragm and lung?

as dark as i am and tryin' to pass
somebody really needs to kick my black ass
for walking like a white man with my rear end tight
but when someone calls me stuffy I'm ready to fight
do I bring it on myself with highfalutin' ways
livin' like whitey did in the brady bunch days?

i been walkin' so long down the other culture's path
that i'm gone need me a little nigga momma wrath
to kick my butt and do it good
the way a nigga momma should
for me paradin' 'round as white
when my skin is shiny as night

as black as I am and tryin' to pass
somebody pleeease kick my black ass

Thus my interest in this chapter is not only in analyzing a literary problem but also in helping to solve a social—even a personal—one.

"Sugaaarrr!" my sister Cookie screamed the half of my nickname that I can't shake. It was my turn to dance a jig, sing a tune, something to entertain the crowd of mostly women and kids gathered in the living room of my apartment. My brothers, male cousins, and brothers-in-law were in the kitchen. I was there too, trying to bond with them, participating in the men-talk they found so enjoyable and that I decided I no longer would avoid. "Sugar Bear!" She wasted no time calling again, this time using my full nickname—the version I like better since "Sugar" alone signifies so much of the effeminacy I hate. Cookie was the only person, family or friend, who was always careful to call me either by my full nickname or just "Bear," rarely only "Sugar"—because "Bear" didn't so easily instigate the taunts that calling me "Sugar" did. "He got sugar in his tank," they used to say as a matter of fact, grownups and kids alike. "He a little sweet, ain't he?" they'd ask my family, mostly my brothers, as if I couldn't hear or answer back, as if I'd tell them I wasn't, which they presumed was a lie.

"Hold your panties," I told Cookie, trying to sound cool or at least get a laugh from one of the guys. But they seemed not to notice. So I just unfolded the paper that I had in my back pocket, waving it as I walked to the living room to indicate that I was doing a reading for my performance, not the modern dance routine that I used to do as my sister Y'shanda sang a Phyllis Hyman or Anita Baker tune in the background after we'd argue about who should be in front—the singer or the dancer. I gave that up at eleven after our last duet at a family reunion or some occasion like that. I had practiced until my routine was perfect, complete with a high kick, twirl, and a frozen pose in the fifth position at the end, with only my fingers moving, wiggling back and forth to affect leaves blowing in the wind. When Tyrone, a proud homosexual, the cousin of somebody's girlfriend, saw my routine, he took it as his cue to outdance me and everyone else at the party with even higher kicks, backbends, and Alvin Ailey leaps. My family egged on a challenge, even though they knew I couldn't outdance Tyrone. Afterward, Tyrone tried to talk to me, pointing out this and that technique, giving me advice about dancing, since he was professionally trained. But I ignored him, because during the competition, when the disco tempo thumped, Tyrone had launched into his jazz dance version of *Swan Lake*. And in between the crowd's "You go, boys," their "Hit its" and "Show 'em whatcha gots," I heard, "Look at that fag" and "Ain't that just like a sissy?" And since I couldn't tell which one of us they were talking about, I pretended to be tired and panted on the sidelines so it wouldn't be me. Tyrone kept right on going, and I admired him, even though I decided right then and there that I wouldn't be caught dead dancing like that again. I didn't want my family to see me as a Tyrone type of person.

After that I limited my performances to lip-synch routines—until that too lost its appeal when I first went to a bar where a drag queen entertainer was lip-synching for a living. I found out that a whole culture and lifestyle revolved around that performance genre and that it was mostly gay. So I never went there again and felt like I was progressing well and fast toward losing the faggot identity that seemed to follow me like a shadow or stick like gum to the bottom of my shoe. Just when I'd turn the corner or scrape it off and walk a few steps, there it was again. And I wasn't about to go conjuring it up—not in the living room of my own apartment, even if there really was no way to avoid it.

I'm reading a poem this year, I announced, clearing my throat—loudly—so if there were any objections I could pretend not to hear them. And I promptly began: "As dark I am and trying to pass."

They roared.

"Somebody needs to kick my black ass."

They howled.

My family, enjoying themselves, participated call-and-response style in the performance. They didn't care so much about the poem's scanty aesthetics, knowing that anyone of them could write one better. My cousin, an amateur rapper and singer, was one of the few men to watch me perform. He was the yearly neighborhood talent show winner; he performed his own material only because his "shit was better than what those jive-ass popular punks did for the white man," as he used to say. Afterward he told me that my poem was off-key. He said it lacked rhythm, that the flow was rough and the language forced, and that he'd show me how to fix it, though he never did, because he was home for only a short time, between trial dates for a murder he said he didn't commit but refused to say who had—a gangbanger's code of ethics or something like that. But what he mostly liked, he told me, and what also seemed to delight the rest of the family, was the man's repeated plea. Every time I got to the refrain, "Somebody needs to . . ." they'd chime in, as if on cue, "kick your black ass." They obviously saw themselves as the poem's community and I, to them, was the failing-to-pass-for-white, dark-skinned black man who needed them to help him get his act together, so he could just be black.

I was inspired to write the poem one night as Marilyn, my sometimes too-white friend, and I talked on the phone. It was a year after I was let go from the nearly all-white school district where she was still teaching. Every weekend she'd call to tell me how much she hated teaching there, though I couldn't figure out why at first. I used to see her as whiter than I could ever be, because she never slipped into the blackness I know. I used to see her whiteness as authentic and mine as made-up, since I had to mold myself so that I could sound and act white proficiently, whereas she just grew up that way, in Tacoma, Washington, in an area heavily populated by white people. Marilyn told me that she and her sister were often the only two blacks at the schools they attended. I met her sister, a fledgling novelist, in and out of college writing programs; she was younger and worse than Marilyn. Too white, some of my family members would say if they met her—Tiger Woods, Tyra Banks white.

Marilyn's sister didn't talk much about black issues or racial politics. She deemed them pointless and outdated and said so once when she was visiting and we all went to dinner. Marilyn and I started joking with each other about who talks the whitest. Her sister playfully rolled her eyes and said, "You guys, people are people." Marilyn and I laughed away our self-consciousness, feeling a little hypocritical, since we are usually the ones to preach her sister's words to others. But when we say it, we mean in the long run, not in the meantime. We know that in this America, even as we've progressed in racial politics, some black people, some who can racially pass for white, still feel it necessary to do so. And some people—like the white wife of Anatole Broyard—still find it necessary to out them. In 1990 Broyard was a seventy-year-old retired "erudite book reviewer for the *New York Times*," whose wife could no longer live a lie or at least she wasn't going to let her husband die with one. So days before he died, she told their college-aged children that their father had black racial heritage (Thadious Davis 1997, xxv). I wonder: If Broyard had been one-eighth Native American, a quarter French, or maybe even half Moroccan, would his wife have been compelled to reveal that part of his secret—to disrupt at death the racial identity he'd chosen?

The literary critic Thadious Davis cites Broyard's experience in her introduction to Larsen's *Passing* as one example of "several recent public revelations of racial passing [that] have revived interest in and speculation about its motives and consequences" (1997, xxiii). The literary critic Mae Henderson suggests that novels about racial passing "educate" readers "ethnographically about black life." She emphasizes that this "renewed interest" stems from "a more general preoccupation with notions of hybridity, biraciality, and social constructionism as they structure contemporary conceptions of personal and social identity" (2002, xx–xxi). In other words, we contemporary readers look to passing novels to help us understand the forces that shape our racial identities—both those ascribed to us and those we avow. Henderson is interested in such questions as, What does it mean to be mixed raced? And how does one with both black and white racial heritages reconcile these identities?

For me, though, these novels address a more fundamental question: Why must blacks still pass? Thadious Davis acknowledges that the answer "is less easy to decipher in the wake of the civil rights movement . . . which led to changes in the legal system" (1997, xxiii). And while Henderson recognizes how central the phenomenon of passing is to ongoing discussions of black racial identity, like Thadious Davis, she cannot account for its endurance. But the anthropologist Signithia Fordham does.

Fordham argues that passing not only persists but is required—not just of blacks with light skin and "good hair" but even of those with nappy hair, wide noses, and skin so black you think maybe it's blue. That is, if they want to achieve success in America's mainstream and elevate their class status.[2] This, of course, includes Marilyn and me. We both are striving to become financially secure, trying to achieve a solidly middle-class status by working in the most mainstream of America's institutions—school—as English teachers, no less. And we both have to do this with our dark skin and kinky hair. But these physical traits don't matter, and it's good for Marilyn and me that they don't, since we could never literally look white. For us, then, "becoming white is not *the* issue" (Fordham 1996, 23). "Acting white" or "looking white on paper—behaving in ways and displaying the skills, abilities, and credentials that were traditionally associated with White Americans"—is what matters because acting white, Fordham stresses, "became the way to pass" after legal discrimination (44).

Fordham's account explains why Marilyn's sister believes that people are just people. As Fordham acknowledges, "acting white is . . . unavoidable," an "inescapable outcome of American citizenship" and "American schooling" (1996, 23). Marilyn's sister may believe that Marilyn and I don't really talk white, that we talk and act American, behaving in ways common to educated people. Her attitude is the result of what the linguist Rosina Lippi-Green points out as "a general unwillingness to accept the speakers of [Black English] and the social choices they have made as viable and functional. Instead we relegate their experiences and capabilities to spheres which are secondary and out of the public eye" (1997, 201). Marilyn's sister refuses to acknowledge the language and cultural differences between blacks and whites, as well as people's negative perceptions about black culture. I believe that, like so many others who hold these views, she wants to excise Black English speakers from the public eye. But even if she doesn't wish to make them invisible, she likely thinks that they experience the problems they do because of their resistance to Americanization. But she's ignoring what Fordham calls the "subtle limitations" of assimilation. In other words, even though Marilyn and I have taken so much advantage of the American dream that we act white in our sleep, we face obstacles that whites don't. And we recognize these limitations in the lives of our black students, particularly when they insist upon using Black English. That's why we haven't chosen to pass as completely as Marilyn's sister has—although we understand that she does it because the psychoemotional pain of negotiating two cultural/racial worlds is far too great for many. For this same reason we understand why there are those, like some of our students, who refuse to pass.

Reflecting on the decision he made to pass for white, the Ex-Colored Man in James Weldon Johnson's *The Autobiography of an Ex-Colored Man* expresses regret, saying: "I feel that I have been a coward, a deserter, and I am possessed by a strange longing for my mother's people" (1995, 99). And, although he says, "My love for my children makes me glad that I am what I am" (100), "an ordinarily successful white man" (99), his gladness cannot replace his anxiety. "I cannot repress the thought," he laments as the novel closes, "that, after all, I have chosen the lesser part, that I have sold my birthright for a mess of pottage" (100). This suggests a simple resolution: If you're unhappy passing for white, just be black. But it's not that easy. In my poem what my family considers to be my white ways have always been or have become just as much a part of me as my black ways. In order for me to be like my family, to return, as it were, to my community, I must not only stop acting white, I must learn how to be black. Because it's impossible for me to recuperate or acquire the necessary blackness, I'm subject to my family's incessant expressions of dissatisfaction.

Similarly, when the Ex-Colored Man announces that he wants "to go back to the very heart of the South, and live among the people," his white patron asks: "What kind of Negro would you make now?" The patron's question is prompted by his perception that the Ex-Colored Man is "by blood, by appearance, by education, and by tastes a white man" (67). It's not the Ex-Colored Man's white skin alone that makes him insufficiently black. What makes the patron exclaim that "this idea you have of making a Negro out of yourself is nothing more than a sentiment" (67) is his conviction that the Ex-Colored Man's behavior, the performance of his racial identity, is sufficiently white.

In *The Mis-Education of the Negro* (1933) Carter G. Woodson sustains the patron's view of whiteness as not only a racial classification but a behavioral one—one that makes it possible for a black man to act white. "When a Negro has finished his education in our schools," Woodson writes, "then, he has been equipped to begin the life of an Americanized or Europeanized white man" (1990, 5). Woodson believes that because of education some blacks inhabit an improper relation to less educated blacks and can therefore be of no assistance to them in their struggle for equality. An educated black person, without the proper consciousness, is no more to underprivileged blacks than your average white man. It's precisely because the Ex-Colored Man's white behaviors are by no means limited to his accent or gait but extend to areas that he cannot manipulate, like education, that his efforts to be black seem futile.

The problem that the Ex-Colored Man and I both face is that we fail to measure up, in ways beyond our control, to what's considered by both whites and blacks to be authentic blackness. Because he has white skin, however, the Ex-Colored Man can escape blackness by completely passing for white—what his patron advises him to do. Passing today, however, no longer mandates that you look white. It requires instead that you be black but act white, erasing the requirement of racial concealment and stressing racial performance.

My poem, then, recasts the significance that Jim Crow placed on skin color with an emphasis on performance. It replaces the light-skinned black who passes by hiding his blackness with a dark-skinned black who passes by performing his whiteness. The danger in both cases is the danger of discovery, although what's discovered isn't exactly the same. In the classic Jim Crow passing saga, such as the *Autobiography*, what's discovered when you're pretending to be white is that you're really black. In my post–Jim Crow passing saga everybody already knows I'm black. My fear is that they'll discover that I'm *really* black—ghetto black, what Chris Rock calls a "nigger." And, of course, in both stories the threat of failure is accompanied by what may be worse—the threat of success. For if I can keep my ghetto blackness from being detected, a move that will keep me estranged from the black community, I risk the same lingering psychoemotional torment that the Ex-Colored Man must bemoan for life.

As another consequence of success the male passer's masculinity and sexuality are inevitably called into question. In his analysis of *Autobiography* Phillip Brian Harper claims the literary passing subject has what he calls a "feminine function," which magnifies the femininity of even male passing characters. This femininity is signified, according to Harper, by the Ex-Colored Man's white racial features.[3] Since passing today involves not looking white but acting white, this femininity is pronounced not by looking white but by the passer's language and behaviors that are racialized as white.

As a boy, especially at that family party, I knew that if I wanted to become fully a part of my black community, to be accepted as black, I also had to comply with the gender behaviors appropriate for my race and sex. Although my poem doesn't explicitly address concepts of masculinity and sexuality that are chained to blackness, I didn't want to put myself at risk of being called a fag. So I read the poem that night in a hip-hop style, trying to connect myself to the more thuggish rap music genre wherein even women refer to each other as man. Thus the post–Jim Crow problem of passing is the drama that my poem presents—the project I know firsthand.

I was hoping that my relatives would see themselves in my poem— see the folly in the performances that blacks are called to give in order to prove our blackness to one another and our whiteness to whites and sometimes our whiteness to blacks and our blackness to whites and how tangled up this gets—and how confusing and frustrating it is. So much so, that we'd go insane if we didn't prevent it, if we didn't choose to live as either a Resisting Black, embracing the performance of blackness while resisting whiteness, like some in my family do, or as a Passing Black, striving toward whiteness and repudiating blackness, as I sometimes do.

"Shuck 'em both," some say, "I'll just be me," trying to find some way to escape race, to keep from identifying themselves as this or that type of black. But they soon find that they have to turn somewhere, perform for some group, before they belong to none, like Leanita Mc-Clain, who grew up in a Chicago ghetto, in the Ida B. Wells housing projects. At only thirty-two, right at the height of a highly successful journalism career, she "took an overdose of a powerful antidepression medicine and went to sleep" (Page 1996, 49).

"I am burdened," she wrote, "with trying to prove to whites that blacks are a people." She was also burdened by her "brothers and sisters," blacks she knew in the hood, "many of [whom] have abandoned me," she said, "because they think that I have abandoned them" (Page 1996, 48). She was called to perform her blackness to keep from becoming estranged, feeling alienated, from the community she felt she belonged to.

Ironically, performing her blackness for whites also made her the success that she was: "I assuage white guilt," she wrote, and "I prove to whites that Blacks are a people." Before she became the first black editorial board member of the *Chicago Tribune,* her blackness had landed her a place at Northwestern University's Medill School of Journalism. Medill wanted to train blacks to meet the media demand, not for light-skinned blacks who were racially passing for white, who couldn't or didn't say they were black, but for blacks who were black, who said it and showed it.

The media didn't want blacks who were too black, though; talking that black talk and acting black—not that kind of black. McClain's "liberal white acquaintances" didn't see her as that type of black anyway. "They pat me on the head," she said, "hinting that I am freak," thinking she was nothing like those in the projects she came from. Because of that she asked the world: "When they attempt to sever me from my own, how can I live with myself?" (Page 1996, 48). McClain got entangled in this racial double bind, called to give one performance to whites and another to blacks. And, inevitably, she gave out, writing: "I will never live long enough to see my people free anyway" (49).

Because McClain was at least three decades removed from separate but unequal and more than one hundred years beyond emancipation from decimation, the Chicago journalist Clarence Page, who writes about his ex-wife's suicide in his essay "Survivors' Guilt," believes she already had the freedom she wanted. "Looking back I see with greater clarity the freedom Leanita had at her disposal, whether she was willing to realize it or not. She did not have to march for it, fight for it, or crusade for it. All she had to do was . . . accept it" (1996, 69).

Page swears that McClain and other middle-class blacks "refuse to see" the freedom that came after Jim Crow, when "anti-discrimination laws made class differences more important arbiters of opportunity than racial differences" (58). He warns that too "many of us compensate by identifying excessively with our less fortunate brethren left behind in the ghetto" (59). Page regards this identification as unnecessary, harmful even, since lower-class blacks post–Jim Crow are separated from middle-class blacks not by race (we're all still black) but by class (some of us are just not poor). Page's confidence in the progress resulting from antidiscrimination laws stems from his comparison of the legal status of blacks before Jim Crow to black class mobility after Jim Crow. But class isn't the only, or even the primary, factor that Page uses to separate blacks.

"Showing your color," Page says, was the term that parents used to foster "the success stories of [his] generation." It "was just another way to say," like Chris Rock, "don't behave like those Negroes, those loud, lazy, godless, shiftless, doo-rag wearing, good-for-nothings who hang out on the corner and get themselves into trouble" (Page 1996, 59). Page fingers the contemporary gangster rappers "Ice T., Ice Cube and Snoop Doggy Dog," who glorify the black ghetto in their lyrics and style of dress, as examples of the types of Negroes he was told not to be like and cautions black people against imitating today. It doesn't matter to Page that Ice T., Ice Cube, and Snoop Doggy Dogg make more money than he does and clearly enjoy greater celebrity. The problem is that they show their color. By advocating that these gangsta rappers hide their color, Page is not saying that they should hide their race, something their dark skin prohibits. He is suggesting that they act white.

Just as the *Autobiography* depicts the Jim Crow project of passing as personified by the nameless protagonist, it predicts the post–Jim Crow project too—embodied by another nameless character: the upper-middle-class black doctor whom the Ex-Colored Man befriends aboard a ship as they travel from Europe to the United States. The doctor invites the Ex-Colored Man to spend a few weeks with him in the Boston area. While they are sightseeing, the doctor points out a group of lower-class blacks that he describes in terms curiously similar to Page's depiction of those who show their color, as "those lazy, loafing, good-for-nothing darkies." The doctor says, "They're not worth digging graves for; yet they are the ones who create impressions of the race." He exclaims to the Ex-Colored Man: "We are the race, and the race ought to be judged by us, not by them" (J. Johnson 1995, 73). Because the doctor's skin is too dark to pass in the way the Ex-Colored Man can, the doctor worries not about whether he should reveal or conceal the fact that he is black but about what blackness is taken to be—how it is defined and by which blacks. The doctor thus transforms the class difference between middle- and lower-class blacks into a racial difference—which ones are truly black?

I argue, then, that the doctor prefigures Page's contempt for lower-class blacks and represents the central problem of black authenticity. Like Johnson's doctor, Page thinks it's the middle class that embodies the race. Like Snoop Doggy Dogg, Ice T., and Ice Cube, my family thinks that being middle class—or, rather, acting middle class—is a way of betraying the race. McClain, pulled in both directions, wanted to reconcile the problem within the race. But neither lower-class blacks (her brothers and sisters in the ghetto), middle-class blacks (Page), nor whites (her colleagues) would allow her to do that. They wanted her to choose—and to prove it through her performance. This is why McClain believed that she would never live to see her people free—because blacks cannot achieve freedom from the burdens of racial performance, unless race ceases to exist as a category of distinction or you die. Knowing the former would not come in her lifetime, McClain hastened the latter.

McClain's racial dilemma and her heroic end uncannily parallels Clare Kendry's in Larsen's *Passing*. In the concluding episode of the novel, Clare's white husband forces his way into an all-black party that she is attending and demands to know if she is "a damned dirty nigger" (1997, 111). Clare frees herself from her husband's demand, and by extension the unspoken demand of the black guests, to claim either her whiteness or her blackness over the other by going through a window. Thadious Davis writes that "were it not for the view of Clare's body" on the ground outside, Clare's "disappearance out the window" could be read "not as death but as escape into a new life" (1997, xxx). However, I read Clare not as escaping into a new life but as choosing, like McClain, to escape the racial limitations of the old one—one where she's forced to choose. As Mae Henderson writes of Clare, "her continued existence would menace both Bellew's [white] and Irene's [black] world, so [since Clare can't be both, she] must cease to exist" (2002, lxxiii). Larsen's ultimate accomplishment in the novel, Henderson says, "lies in the narrative performance of her refutation of essentialism" (lxxiv). But in jumping to her death, in refusing to choose either blackness or whiteness, Clare isn't just refusing essentialism. Neither is she embracing a performative account of race. *She's refusing to perform.* From this perspective it's clear why Thadious Davis and Henderson can't explain why passing continues—because what's wrong with Henderson's antiessentialism is that it produces the demand for racial performance. Essentialism begets essentialism, even if we call it antiessentialism.

Like McClain and Clare, I want to be free from the burdens of racial performance, free from having to choose a passing identity or a resisting one, free from having to be this kind of black here, that kind there. I'm tired of being the family fag who tries to prove he's a man, of being the white boy, the academic scapegoat, the one who's book smart but not street smart, who's always running up behind white folks like a whipped puppy, sorry eyes, wet nose, and all, wagging for affection, hoping they'll accept me for who I am, asking them to forgive me when my blackness offends them.

I'm tired of seeing little black kids, too smart for their own good, who got it right, but their right is made their wrong, when they call school white and hate it. There's nothing left if their names are not Iverson, Shaq, or Jay-Z. The future is grave for them, because many of them end up in one, in jail, or on the streets, on drugs, and still poor, and they think it's okay, the way it should be: a cashier at the lo cal burger joint at forty; on welfare at seventeen with one, maybe two, kids and pregnant again; a gas station attendant; a security guard at the local Chinese-owned clothing store, stealing a jersey here, a pair of sneakers there to make herself feel better. "Jobs somebody has to do," people say to make it seem like race is not the issue and point to white people who are in the same boat. But why does it have to be mostly black people?

Racial discrimination is now illegal, but performance discrimination that is based on that once-lawful, now fallacious, biologically mistaken, racist, though still race-concept-informing rule that rendered anyone black who had one or more drops of black blood, is not. Because of this concept we're called to perform our racial identities and should resist rather than conform.

But when Cookie came up at the end of my reading and kicked me smack dab in the rear end, and when my family's applause and cheers grew louder, entertained more by her performance than my poem, I knew they didn't get it. If they had, I wouldn't have been the only one getting kicked that night.

NIGGA-GENDER

That black men who display hypermasculine characteristics fetishize—that is, simultaneously love and loathe—those considered less masculine or, to be explicit, that niggas covet faggots, has been unmasked in insightful criticism.[1] That faggots desire to be niggas has occasioned less critique, which is one of the reasons I disclose my own example here. In this chapter I want to merge these conversations in order to discuss black males' willing and coerced collusion with the performances that the terms *nigga* and *faggot* signify. The racial performance critic E. Patrick Johnson illustrates what I mean by revealing his own collusion.

As part of his study of the performance and politics of blackness, Johnson conducts an ethnographic interview with his grandmother, Mary Rhyne, about her life as a live-in domestic. Because of his familial relationship with Rhyne, his response to her narrative was not exclusively academic but was rightly intimate and familiar. Yet he placed deliberate limits on his personal communication. He acknowledges that when the opportunity arose to discuss his sexuality, he avoided coming out as a homosexual to his grandmother. Instead he allowed his silence to project what he calls his "performance of heterosexuality" (2003, 112).

But E. Patrick Johnson doesn't always perform heterosexuality. In fact, some of his younger gay friends refer to him as "mother" because, as he writes, "they admire how I lead my life as an openly gay man." He continues, "Because they are still somewhat closeted, they aspired to be as comfortable as I am in my sexuality" (2003, 93). However comfortable Johnson may be in his sexuality among his friends, in his classroom, and in his scholarship, where these details are disclosed, he's not as comfortable in his grandmother's home, where his performance of heterosexuality endures. He writes: "I never (and still have not) revealed my sexual orientation to my grandmother" (2003, 112).

What compels Johnson to be so out as an academic yet so reserved within a major domain of the black home? He and Rhyne are the best people—and probably together—to provide a reply. As it is, Johnson leaves the matter open, not so much, I think, for others to settle but because he's vulnerable to the burden of racial performance. I'm not writing to further impose this burden on him. I use his specific example to illustrate the gender problem inherent in the linguistic conflicts that exist between the metaphorical sites of school and home. I also use his example to provide a framework for asking the questions that drive this chapter: Why is language taken as a projection of sexuality? Is it more accepted and expected for black men to be homosexual in academic settings? Do school and home really require black men to put on contradictory displays of masculinity? If school and home demand conflicting gender performances, how do black males use language and silence to enact these roles? What benefits result from embracing these performances? And, what are the consequences of resisting them?

I begin to answer these questions by rehearsing the gender performance I gave at my brother's house, where I desired to be seen as more masculine, less as a faggot and more as a nigga. The narrative that follows recounts that interaction. By discussing my own masculine angst along with analyzing the anxiety expressed by E. Patrick Johnson and other black male academics, I hope to shed light on how the burden of racial performance produces social and linguistic pressures that coerce us to give conflicting gender performances and force us into categories like niggas and faggots.

I headed to my brother's house with two of my friends, Michelle and Rianne, ready to party. We had planned to stay an hour, maybe less. Just long enough to eat and to check out his pad before making our way to club yet-to-be-decided. This meant that we'd barhop until we found the right crowd, right music, and right vibe. We sought eclectic racial diversity, infused with bourgeois blackness, and topped with just enough ghetto blackness—enough to keep us grounded, enough to grab in case we needed to bust somebody over the head with it, the way we've never done but are ready to do anytime or anywhere for that matter. We weren't worried; none of this would be hard to find on a Saturday night in Chicago. So the brief detour to my brother's place for his year-too-late housewarming party didn't funk up our prospects.

I was reluctant to ask Michelle and Rianne to come with me or, to be more honest, I was embarrassed, especially since my brother lives on the notorious West Side. Although that's where we all grew up, Michelle now lives in one of the oldest and perhaps most posh suburbs of Chicago, and Rianne lives in a brand spanking new townhome near a university—in the exclusive gated neighborhood that her architect husband helped design. We're all wannabe black bourgeoisies, or, to use Momma's word, sadiddy (that's black for you think you too good to come back to the hood).

Y'shanda told me about our brother's party in an oh-by-the-way fashion because she didn't think I would go. She had already made up her mind to stay home. She was pregnant and perhaps paranoid because of it. She said she wasn't going anywhere or doing anything that might jeopardize her condition. Her decision surprised me since she used go back to the projects at all times of the day and night to visit our oldest sister and our aunt. She's always saying, "Family has to stick together." And if nobody else is, she's determined to be the glue.

She used to drag her gangbanger-turned-University-of-Chicago-master's-degreed Puerto Rican husband along, perhaps for protection, and strut on to the projects, with each of them holding the hand of one of their two lightly toasted girls, who always had their "good" hair done up in pigtails. Y'shanda says she doesn't, but I think she combs their hair that way so as not to offend their girl cousins who have just enough hair to snap into something some might call a ponytail. Y'shanda used to try to convince me to go back to the projects with her. She'd say that it was safer now. "Just keep your eyes open," she'd say mother-style, as if to say: "Just look both ways before you cross the street." But I would ask her in signifying fashion if God made her eyes bulletproof.

Tonight, though, I was asking her, trying all I could to convince her to come along. "It can't be as unsafe as the projects, can it? His neighborhood has single-family homes and two-flats, right?" I used this architecturally informed racial reasoning that was left over from my high school days, when I used to get off the bus a block or two out of the way, south of where I was supposed to, on Washington Street, instead of Lake Street, because the projects, at least from Western to Damen, didn't border that street, and you couldn't see them from the bus.

But, as they say, you can fool some of the people, but I was fooling none of the kids who rode as far as I did. They all knew I lived in the projects. And one day they told me they couldn't figure out why I was lying about it. But if they knew I lived there, then they also knew why I was pretending to live somewhere else. I lied because I didn't want to be teased. If you lived in the projects, it was said your momma was on welfare and exchanging her food stamps for green dollars to buy alcohol or drugs. It was said that you were probably dumb and got into the mostly white, highest-ranking high school in Chicago only because the principal at your elementary school thought you were a nice kid, though not quite smart enough, and called her principal friend to let you in on the promise of a payback. My friends who rode the bus with me lived in either a single-family home or in one of the two- or three-flat buildings near the projects. If you lived in one of these, you were considered to be a step above project people, which was all that was needed to be considered two steps closer to middle class. My friends who wanted me to get off at Lake Street, to embrace having grown up in the projects, didn't have to deal with their scorn and laughter, or their misplaced pity, or what I read as their false sympathy.

Y'shanda went to the rival high school, Whitney Young, which in those days vied for the top spot with Lane Technical High School, where I was enrolled. She too, but not as often as I, told friends she lived other places—one or two blocks away from the projects, where it was not thought to be as bad but was anyway, which we were all willing to ignore to keep divisions divided, because we all benefit from them. This is the way identity works. So she understood my reasoning, but it made no impression. She'd already made up her mind not to go to the party and told me in her big sister way that the case was closed.

With or without her I decided to go, though I was thinking it would have been better if she'd come. After all, she is the family mediator, a role I knew would be needed at my brother's house—the brother with whom I hadn't spoken in a good year and a half, perhaps two—could be three if I actually cared to count. It didn't matter that we lived less than twenty minutes from each other because it wasn't spatial distance that kept us apart.

When we were younger, he relentlessly called me a fag anywhere and everywhere, indoors, outdoors, in front of his friends, in front of mine, didn't matter. "Get your faggot butt upstairs," he'd say during those rare occasions when Momma would let us go outside to play or when we'd sneak out when she was at work. On other occasions, when I was jumping rope, playing hopscotch, or enjoying some other game said to be only for girls, he'd disown me when his friends would say, "Hey, man, ain't that your little brother?"

"Hell, no," he'd respond.

"Yes, I am," I'd yell, pretending my heart didn't sink each time from the rejection. Even when I tried to play basketball, curse, and fight like the other boys, like I thought he wanted me to, it made no difference. That's when I began to imagine him invisible, nonexistent, a stranger to be tolerated, avoided even, as someone not to be spoken to unless absolutely necessary. If our apartment had caught fire and he was in it, I would've refused to warn him—even if God had tried to make me. That's the distance we couldn't travel.

However, there I was that night, heading to his house. Michelle and Rianna were cool with going when I told them we could drink and eat for free before clubbing. I told them nothing of the strained relationship, but I'm sure they sensed something strange since I rarely mention male members of my family. This is partly because my father is more of a stranger than a daddy, a person I've met a few times but who has never quite made it to the acquaintance stage. My oldest brother is a hefty twelve years older; we never quite bonded, though he's always been my supporter—a real rooter for me in academic studies. He's the one who used to call me Professor Wally Ford—one word like *Walliford*—fast like—when I was younger and still does because he said I remind him of a professor/doctor on one of the soaps—*All My Children,* I think. He calls it his wish for me, my self-fulfilling prophecy—to become a professor.

Then there's the brother in question. He's maybe ten years older than I am. And then there's the third older brother who's eight years older and who grew up in Detroit. His daddy took him away when he was three to visit his grandmother and never brought him back. "My boy ain't growing up in no projects," he told Momma by phone once he got there. She said she cried a little but sent the birth certificate and social security card because it was the best thing to do at the time. Between him and me there are three girls, Y'shanda, who's two and a half years older, and Cookie, who's three and half years older, maybe four. Latonya, who's five or six years older and now lives in Burlington, Iowa, is somewhat like my brothers to me. We never really clicked. My oldest sister, Bell, is eleven years older. Y'shanda and Cookie and I, we're the tight ones. They're the ones I mostly talk about—them and Momma.

As we drove to my brother's house, we talked about which club we would hit first and mapped out a plan and route: all the free clubs first, then on to the least expensive, hoping we'd find something we like so we could save money. If not, then we'd go to the bars with ten to twelve dollar drinks, where we knew we'd wind up anyway. We had to experience our middle class–ness to the fullest extent possible, like it was a novelty, like we'd lose it tomorrow but didn't care if we did, because we'd have a good time tonight. We had to lay down the twelve dollars for a vodka gimlet, Chopin and Roses, thank you, just because we could and to say we had. Experiencing this with each other was of no small consequence—somehow we made it real for the other—we confirmed for one another that although we're one step from the ghetto, we'd never let the other go back.

We debated, just for fun, how much money we were willing to spend and who owed whom what from last time, who bought the last round and at which bar—all as we drove deep into the West Side and onto a crevice that we joked the city had the nerve to call a street. We noticed that some teenage boys had put up a basketball court right in the middle of the block and just kept right on playing, undisturbed, as we drove up, at night, on a street that had no street lamps. They lighted their game with the headlights of a car that also blasted groove music; I remember thinking it was much too slow and loud for playing ball. There were other boys who were not yet playing. "The glarers," Rianne called them, meshing her English PhD training for condensing people and experiences into neat terms with her black culturally learned sensibility for naming. The glarers, she theorized, were watching for cars, meeting the eyes of drivers and daring. She advised that I not challenge. But I'm a black PhD too, and even if I weren't, I knew to make the U-turn without a fuss and to pretend that I was happy about going three blocks the long way around to get to my brother's old-new house.

As we parked the car, Michelle, drawing on her undergraduate training in sociology, commented that the city had forced zoned parking on the neighborhood because Mayor Daley, like his father, wanted to get all he could from poor blacks. "Daley knows," she said, "that the city will collect plenty of money from tickets given to visitors who won't take time to notice the 'Permit Parking Only' signs and from towing the cars of residents who might themselves forget there are restrictions on parking in front of their own homes." We laughed even harder in spite of ourselves and walked into my brother's house, which I thought, probably because of our past, looked like he should have been throwing a party to move out of. I felt bad, though, when I saw a faint look of despair on his face when I asked, "How long have you been living here? Only a year? It looks like you've been here at least twen . . . uh . . . two years." I bit my tongue on "twenty," but I think he heard it anyway.

I didn't want to insult my brother. I was nervous about what I had come to do. I was there to break the silence, to come out to my brother, to expose myself as a nigga, which meant I had to shed the faggot facade that he, in part, had forced me to adopt. According to the discourse of black racial authenticity that my brother speaks, faggots are utterly juxtaposed to niggas. The superstar rapper Ice Cube configures this gender contrast in his oft-cited pithy formulation, "Real niggas ain't faggots." Like my brother, Cube denounces faggot-gender in order to secure his nigga masculinity. His statement constitutes an enactment of the nigga-gender he seeks. Yet his proclamation fortifies the burden he unsuccessfully tries to weaken. Each time he chooses nigga-gender, he must recommit to proving he's not a faggot. He must recycle the language and behavior that reconstitute his gender. Those who embrace or who are ascribed faggot-gender are subject to the same pressure. We must ceaselessly prove that we're not niggas. In both cases our efforts intensify the burden that we wish to alleviate, but they also produce an ironic and overwhelming desire for the other.

I take my brother's performance at the housewarming party, where we were friendly but cautious, distant yet cordial, as proof of his desire. He bragged to our cousins and to his childhood friends who were also present, telling them that I'm the family professor, a PhD. He told them I'm the one who doesn't have to work as hard as he does, driving a city bus on the graveyard shift, then going straight to work as a store manager just to make ends meet. He said he heard from Momma or somebody that I stay home and write—all day—about God knows what, essays that nobody he knows ever reads. But ain't it something, he asked, that I get paid to do it? I read strained efforts toward reconciliation in his comments—efforts I appreciate. But more obvious was his insistence that I get to do all that he finds admirable because I'm a fag, and his friends and he don't because they're not. And underneath that was an apology, an excuse for my faggotry and a justification for his friends' and his niggahood.

What my brother finds enviable about me is to him not only a function of our gender difference but also a function of our perceived class difference. Really, the two are inextricably linked. My (nigga) gender insufficiency is offset, though not entirely, by what he sees as the leisure, comfort, and ease of white-collar work, especially that of a university intellectual. There are certain privileges he sees in my being a faggot, privileges he covets for himself. This allows him to give me tacit approval. He believes I'm at least milking my gender for all it's worth, but the benefits I reap aren't appealing enough to get him to barter what he believes I've had to trade—not just the correct gender identification but a proper racial one. For him what it costs to increase my class status is just not worth what's gained.

Cube's statement that I quoted earlier is also an expression of class or, rather, a statement against the black middle-class ideology popularized by the likes of Bill Cosby and Shelby Steele. Cube seems to say to his listeners, "You don't have to identify with whites to increase your class status, and you don't have be a faggot, either." There is a bit of irony in his advice, of course, since he is a middle-class dude who is not from the hood. But his advice is readily believed because he pretends he's from the ghetto, is handsomely paid to be a nigga, and offers a gender performance that challenges the American educational system, which says niggas will not succeed. Cube also challenges the conservative black middle class, which admittedly embraces whiteness and the attendant racial and gender restrictions that it imposes. And further, as a result of accepting these restrictions, this segment of the black middle class seems more and more ready to indulge its insatiable craving for censuring anything and everything associated with or representative of the black lower class, which fuels the conflict that Cube's words exemplify.

My own envy of Cube is certainly, but not entirely, about class. I have a good deal of education, yet I will make in ten years what he probably spends out of his surplus in a day. I often wonder what it's like to be able to capitalize on black masculinity the way he does. This is not to say that he doesn't have talent. That he does is more than evident. But he also has what I'm considered to be missing metaphorically. He has balls. I have brains. He generates wealth. I produce information. It's no wonder that my brother identifies with Cube—because with his two jobs he likely makes way more than I do. What would my brother do with the books that academics publish—books like this one that, while sometimes are about him, rarely, if ever, address him?

Thus he safeguards his balls and treasures their benefits. Because I enjoy the modicum of envy that I get from my brother, I don't tell him that I too moonlight, that I have to teach extra classes at the local community college, and I certainly won't tell him about my working the late shift as a cashier at the video store that one of my white students manages. Then what would I have? I guess I still might have the wider everyday social cachet, the regular association with white people that my brother eschews. But if he has to encounter the obstacles and hidden racism that I have to deal with, it's likely he'll think, "What's the point?" So, yes, I'm also jealous of my brother. If I were rich or even solidly middle class, in a higher income bracket than my brother, I would still envy him—and Cube. My wish would remain. I'd desire to be masculine. Of course, I'm not the only one. The Harvard law professor Randall Kennedy offers his own confession that reflects this point.

In his book *Nigger* Kennedy acknowledges that what attracts him to black comedians and rappers like Ice Cube "who use and enjoy [the word] nigger" is not that they're famous or even rich. For him it's that they "care principally, perhaps exclusively, about what they themselves think, desire, and enjoy—which is part of their allure. Many people (*including me*)," Kennedy writes, "are drawn to these performers despite their many faults because, among other things, they exhibit a bracing independence" (2002, 171; emphasis added).

This "bracing independence" is synonymous with the very masculinity that constitutes nigga-gender—a point that Kennedy implies but that the writer Gloria Naylor explains. In "Mommy, What Does 'Nigger' Mean?" Naylor recounts the positive validation of masculinity that *nigger* signified when she was a girl. She writes that "a woman could never be a 'nigger' in the singular, with its connotations of confirming worth," and when *nigger* was used in the plural to include women, the term took a misogynistic and pejorative turn. "It became a description of some group within the community," Naylor says, "that had overstepped the bounds of decency" like "parents who neglected their children" or "a drunken couple who fought in public," or "people who simply refused to look for work." And even then the masculine glory of *nigger* itself wasn't spoiled because such people were referred to as "trifling niggers" (1994, 345–46).

As an expression of honor or praise, as an individual affirmation of character, the term *nigger* was reserved for "a man," Naylor writes, "who had distinguished himself in some situation that brought [the community's] approval for his strength, intelligence or drive." Or, "when used with a possessive adjective by a woman—'my nigger'—it became a term of endearment for husband or boyfriend." Nigger, then, as Naylor describes it, "became *the pure essence of manhood*—a disembodied force that channeled their past history of struggle and present survival against odds into a victorious statement of being" (1994, 345; emphasis added).

And just as the comedians and rappers whom Kennedy admires disregard the perception of whites who are more apprehensive about blacks' use of *nigger/nigga* than their own, so do the folks whom Naylor describes. They "took a word that whites used to signify worthlessness or degradation and rendered it impotent," Naylor says. "They transformed 'nigger' to signify the varied and complex human beings they knew themselves to be" (1994, 345). This disregard not only applies to white perceptions but is also directed toward those influential blacks like Oprah Winfrey and Cornel West who have called for, in West's words, "a moratorium on the term" (West 2001b). In effect, current users of *nigger/nigga* say to whites and other blacks who disagree with them, as Kennedy writes, "I don't give a fuck" (2002, 170).

This phrase is infamous and carries currency among black males, especially those who claim nigga-gender. It's seductive, enticing, but also misleading. It cloaks in cool just how much of a fuck they give. What the phrase "I don't give a fuck" really does is convert racial and gender anxiety into a mask of nonchalance. That niggas carry it off so well, however, is exactly why Kennedy and I are drawn to them. As college professors, we're forced into linguistic constraints that restrict our blackness and masculinity. Whereas rappers exaggerate their blackness and masculinity, we are required to underplay ours. Phillip Brian Harper describes the dilemma in terms of speech and silence: "Black people's successful participation in modes of discourse validated in mainstream culture—their facility with Received Standard

English, for instance—actually implicates them in a profound *silence* regarding their African American identity" (1996, 7). But make no mistake about it: This silencing of blackness and masculinity in predominantly white contexts is not the result of being forbidden to use BEV only as a dialect. Few blacks, if any, use it exclusively, and black professors and professionals perhaps even less so. Instead, this silence is marked by our being encouraged and sometimes required to remain distant, separated from the political concerns and cultural practices of the black lower class. In this sense BEV becomes synonymous with expressing that which we're required to suppress in white contexts.

Johnson's ethnographic interview with his grandmother that I mention at the outset glosses this racial point and exposes the gender and sexual implications connected to it. As part of his study Johnson also interviews his grandmother's long-term former employer, to whom he refers as "Mrs. Smith." About that exchange Johnson writes: "I found it difficult to remain silent when hearing [Smith] refer to my grandmother as a 'mammy.' The interview was one moment in the process where my role as an academic/ethnographer transcended, to the point of silence, my role as grandson/black American" (2003, 112). The detached role of the stereotypical academic compelled Johnson to silence his desire to speak out against racist typecasting of black women, of his grandmother, no less. To my mind, correcting Smith would have been a reasonable attempt not only to educate her about injurious racist language but to protect his grandmother from it. But none of this happened because Johnson probably wanted to spare his grandmother the antagonism that might have arisen between her and her former employer. He also likely wanted to avert the personal consequences that he faced himself. What were those consequences?

Calling Smith out had the very real potential to color perceptions of Johnson as a scholar and characterize him as someone who is too angry, who takes the history of race relations too personally. And would not this profile further color him as a "nigger" to someone who called his grandmother "mammy"? His collusion, then, was an act of self-protection, protecting his academic and professional image by giving a racial and gender performance that identified him as a nonthreatening black man.

Johnson's silence about his racial concerns suppresses for Smith exactly what his silence regarding his homosexuality expresses for his grandmother. As a way of contextualizing the moments when his sexuality was at issue, he reports that one of his grandmother's neighbors was a gay white man about whom she made disparaging remarks. Johnson says he condoned the comments and even allowed her to discard baked goods the man made for him during his stay. "My silence about my queerness," he writes, "implicated me in my grandmother's sometimes homophobic, sometimes ambivalent, attitude towards . . . homosexuality in general" (2003, 112). Johnson's silence with his grandmother allowed him to be seen as man enough and black enough, whereas his performance with Smith prevented him from being seen as too black and perhaps hypermasculine. What's behind this paradox?

As Johnson's example clearly shows, identifying with the racial concerns of blacks is another way of speaking black language, and both are principal ways of performing black manhood. This helps explain why so many men respond to the confines placed around black speech as an effort to suppress their expression of blackness and stifle their masculinity. Black men who comply with these restrictions are perceived as being nonthreatening and as a result may experience a measure of success in professional and academic environments, where such restrictions are often imposed. The problem, of course, is that these men must often contend with being perceived as unmanly—indeed, they're seen as failing to be men—a performance that is understood to express homosexuality. From this perspective the masculine anxiety that Johnson experienced around his grandmother appears to have less to do with his actual sexuality and more to do with his fear of being perceived as inadequately masculine, as less than a man.

What's tricky but true about this configuration is that being deemed inadequately masculine is tantamount to being judged a homosexual. One is taken as the signifier of the other. Being homosexual, then, doesn't exempt one from the masculine fear that other black men face at the thought of being considered gay—because what's beneath the anxiety is the concern of being perceived as insufficiently masculine, as unmanly. Perhaps the unique problem for black homosexuals is that they must contend with their sexuality's being taken as the very confirmation of a notion that arises from a racist society.

Because Johnson's silence functions differently in a white context with Smith than it does in the black context with Rhyne, his performance may appear to underscore an erroneous assumption: that because whites feel more relaxed around a nonthreatening black man, they have no need to feel anxious about his sexuality, whereas blacks are preoccupied with homosexuality because it calls black manhood into question. But, really, whites' comfort with nonthreatening black men stems from the belief that the sexual threat that black men are thought to carry as a sheer result of our race is eradicated by our performance. Our sexuality is always at issue, which is perhaps why blacks respond so vigorously to the question of manhood.

It's important to note, however, that these and like views on racial performance and sexuality cannot be easily reduced to a matter of mere black versus white. In fact, some whites may accept the use of BEV and what it represents racially before many blacks will—even blacks who speak it themselves. And some whites who impose restrictions on black speech may, ironically, view black men who accept these requirements as being inadequately black and insufficiently masculine. And blacks who embrace the linguistic limits on BEV, because they believe that doing so provides access to success in the mainstream, may also promote the use of BEV with other blacks because of what it represents racially and sexually. All this is implied in the dilemma that Johnson exemplifies. And his duplicity marks the gender and racial paradox that black men must consistently contend with through racial performance.

The risk that black professionals take in identifying too closely with the struggles of the people is also illustrated in Harper's recounting of the occasion when the newscaster "[Max] Robinson became the center of controversy." Harper writes that "[Robinson] was reported telling a college audience that the various network agencies, including ABC, discriminate against their journalists, and that the news media in general constitute 'a crooked mirror' in which 'white America views itself.'" For saying this he was "summoned to the offices of then ABC News president Roone Arledge," where Robinson "perform[ed]," what Harper calls, "a type of rhetorical backstep" (1996, 7). Harper quotes a *New York Times* story about the flap, which reported that Robinson said he "had not meant to single out ABC for criticism."

Although Robinson rescinds his remark for the sake of his job, Harper contends the retraction doesn't function so much as an annulment of his critique but as a deliberate rhetorical maneuver characteristic of BEV, a move called "louding" or "loud-talking"—which Harper defines as a technique whereby a subordinate black interlocutor speaks loud enough that the intended audience overhears the words but cannot respond directly to what was said. In other words, when loud-talking blacks are confronted for some indirect but intended insult, the black interlocutor can reply, Harper says, "Oh, I wasn't talking to you" (1996, 9).[2]

Loud-talking in the context of Harper's analysis is a feature of BEV, but it is not one I promote or celebrate. This kind of sneak-speaking, of not being able to address race directly, of being silenced on institutionally unauthorized issues of injustice, transforms BEV into a subversive strategy, a clandestine linguistic practice that turns its speakers into veritable tricksters. It seems that while blacks are discouraged from using BEV, we are at the same time put in racially dangerous situations that necessitate its use for survival. It also seems that Robinson's ultimate goal of exposing continued forms of oppression is mitigated by the requirement of the "rhetorical backstep." Indeed, lawyers, newscasters, professors, and professionals who write about the plight of blacks and who seek the black masses as part of their primary audience are often ridiculed, reprimanded into silence, or asked to backstep their efforts, as in the case involving Cornel West that Robinson's example anticipates.

West, who held one of the highest-ranking positions that a university professor could attain, was summoned to the office of Harvard president Lawrence Summers and, according to Martin Van Der Werf, a writer for the *Chronicle of Higher Education*, was "berated" for recording a rap CD, *Sketches of My Culture*. In self-defense Summers says he was interested in discussing "excellence in scholarship and the upholding of high standards" (Van Der Werf 2002, A29). After West went public about the meeting, it was Summers who loud-talked, who danced the rhetorical backstep, likely because of West's academic superstar status. In his apology Summers uttered some mumbo jumbo—nothing as eloquent as the louding of BEV—about his intent. He said, "I regret any faculty member leaving a conversation feeling they are not respected. That is never my intent. . . . I would never want a faculty member to leave one of our conversations feeling mistreated or misunderstood" (Van Der Werf 2002, A30).[3] Even so, that West's CD came up as a contentious topic, when he is also author of numerous scholarly monographs and essays and at the time was working on more, pinpoints the imposition of silence that we black academics and professionals experience when identifying with issues that concern everyday blacks, in speaking about and for them, in recognizing their situation as part of our own.

What's more is that, unlike Robinson's, West's message in *Sketches* doesn't spotlight institutional racism. Instead, his focus is entirely on how self-help can assist blacks in overcoming obstacles. And, further, on the matter of using the word *nigger*, West croons that it interferes with the goals of democracy. He sings in the song "N-Word" that blacks should stop using the term because "it associates black people with being inferior, subhuman and subordinate" (2001b). Thus he rhapsodizes to consumers of rap music, who include the black lower class, versions of the considerations that Summers says he wished to discuss with West: self-interrogation, reevaluation of cultural practices, and increased value in education.

Despite these overlaps, West was chastised not only by Summers but also by Shelby Steele, who has written on self-help in overcoming racial problems. Steele absolutely eschews blacks who claim to be victims of racial oppression. He believes they manufacture obstacles for themselves that impede their progress. "Stop blaming the white man all the time" is a way to characterize his main message. This is also part of the message that West promotes on his CD, although he is less acerbic than Steele is known to be. What really led Summers and Steele to disregard the fact that West's message is one they themselves preach is that West's rap CD disrupts the fallacious notion that the behaviors and interests of BEV speakers and WEV speakers are diametrically opposed. Or, in this case, that West's status as professor inherently and necessarily separates him from lower-class blacks.

But this is a separation that Steele is committed to. Like me, Steele has spent his entire life running from the lower class in order to secure his position among the black middle class—a class that he says "has always defined its class identity by means of positive images gleaned from middle- and upper-class white society and by means of negative images of lower class blacks" (1990, 99a). Steele's disidentification with the black lower class resulted from images that he said "amounted to a negative instruction manual in class identity" (1990, 99a). The protagonist of this manual, of course, is Steele himself; the antagonist is a character named Sam, who, according to Steele, was the personification of all that he despised and "did not want to be" (1990, 99a). Steele and I both know well the one rule that comprises the instruction manual: in order to become middle class you must not only cease to be lower class, you must also become an ex-nigger.

Imitating whites and repudiating those blacks who are considered niggers are requisite to middle-class status. This is because the black lower class is the personified depository for the immorality and wickedness that occurs among other/upper classes and within other races. It's necessary for the black lower class to represent the site of debauchery in order to justify condemning it and, in Steele's and my case, leaving it. In other words, the class difference has to be identifiably distinct—particularly socially and linguistically—since there's no way to distinguish one class from the other racially or economically, given the financial success of rappers and those who glorify the lower class.

From all this the problem is clear: Steele, who writes, "I have often felt myself *contriving* to be black" (1990, 106), is faced not only with the threat of insufficient racial identification but also, and perhaps more important, with the threat of a failed manhood. This is just too much to bear—and in the university, where Steele thought he was safe. It's understandable, then, why Steele rebukes West and why he encourages whites to engage blacks in "more imbroglios like the one that happened between Summers and West" (2002, A18). It's an attempt by a victim of racial (masculine) performance to alleviate his burden by imposing it on others. If more whites, who carry the power in universities, agree with Steele, they can stop those like West whose performance brings the threat of insufficient racial identification and insufficient masculine identification. But the burden continues. West went to Princeton.

For West's part, although he doesn't advocate the use of the term *nigger*, his "bracing independence," as indicated by his response to Summers's complaint, that he won't "tolerate disrespect, dishonor, and the devaluing" of his self-worth by a white man (Thulani Davis 2002), makes him, according to all of Naylor's requisites, a nigger/ nigga. In fact, this is what makes West a success. Unlike so many of us, he can produce just enough authenticity and enough pimp walk to pass as black without succumbing to the plight of the black lower class.

My brother isn't ever going to be a Cornel West and neither am I. So we're limited to trying to be just like each other in the different contexts of home and school, which is what I did at my brother's, where my performance was something of a success. I mean, I had dressed the part, with the low-hanging, baggy pants that showed designer boxer shorts. I had on a sports cap and even practiced my pimp walk. I was ready. I dressed like this not only to perform nigga-gender but so that Michelle and Rianne wouldn't be considered fag hags. I knew that in order to really secure my gender performance, they had to be considered potential sexual partners, not just friends. This is an aspect of my performance that is hardest to admit. I used them that night, in that moment, for my own selfish, masculine purpose. And it worked. When I talked to my brother's friends, some of them asked, out of Michelle's and Rianne's earshot, "You fucking them, li'l bro?" When I just fixed my lips in some kind of coy-boy grin, they took that as a yes or at least an "I'm going to try." They laughed loud and said, "Way to go, nigga." I just beamed. Glad to be a nigga and ignoring the cost to Michelle and Rianne.

I enjoyed being a nigga so much that our expected one hour stay turned into two, turned into three, until Michelle absolutely insisted that we go to her favorite spot before it closed. But when we got there, I was turned away for wearing a ball cap. When I took it off, the bouncer looked down and said, "Sorry, no sneakers." We went to another club and I was told my jeans were too baggy and also that my coat was too big. And since I'd never really dressed like this before to go clubbing, we were somewhat surprised and decided that I should just go home and change. I reclad myself in a pair of leather slacks and a 1970s disco shirt that had a long, flared collar. I topped off the getup with some expensive ostrich skin shoes that Michelle had picked out for me at Barney's New York, the one in Chicago, when we'd gone shopping on Rush Street a month or so before.

We went back to Michelle's spot and got in without a hitch. As soon as we entered, we began dancing in a three-person Soul Train line; one danced in the middle as the other two watched, clapping and swinging. Other clubbers joined our line; I let Michelle and Rianne do most of the dancing, while I held two candles above their heads. I was happy, moving freely, unconscious of my earlier performance. I had done enough of that for one night. But no sooner had it slipped my mind than I was brought right back in it. One black male standing at the bar with a white male blurted out "he's gay" loud enough for me to hear. Then the black guy made a point of saying "faggot" in my direction as he and his friend walked slowly by. Michelle and Rianne looked at me, expecting me to get macho as they've seen me do before, or they might have been looking for my signal so they could get macho, as they've done before. But I just kept right on dancing, pretending, as I used to, that I was undisturbed. I was over my capacity for dealing with racial performance, and I didn't want it to interfere with my fun. But how could it not? It has been, after all, interfering with my entire life.

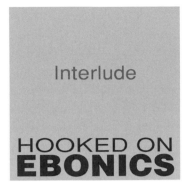

Interlude

HOOKED ON
EBONICS

I am often of two minds when members of the black underclass, "the lower economic people," as the comedian Bill Cosby recently called them, are chastised for their speech, their behaviors—their failure, according to Cosby, in "not holding up their end in [the civil rights] deal."[1] With one mind I believe that poor blacks could do more for themselves by taking better advantage of educational and other opportunities. With the other mind I see the many obstacles that block their way, that prevent them from realizing their dreams. The irony of this double-mindedness, however, is that it produces a certain clarity, not about which to choose—whether to side with Cosby or those he scolds—but about how views like Cosby's are inevitable in our racialized society.

In this interlude I want to briefly meditate on Cosby's statement and connect his words to some of what I said in part 1, that is, why I want to be white and why I and other black men sometimes fetishize one another—and sometimes want to destroy each other. Because the purpose of this interlude is to mark my intellectual shift in this book from the personal, from "Home," to the professional and theoretical, to "School," I also want to place Cosby's discussion, to which I return in the last chapter, within the larger context of race and language.

In his speech, given on the occasion of the fiftieth anniversary of *Brown v. Board of Education* (hereafter *Brown*),[2] Cosby categorically castigates the black underclass because, as he told the crowd, "these people are not parenting. . . . They are buying things for the kid—$500 sneakers." He then asks, "For what?" To him the parents should spend more wisely; they could "spend $250 on 'Hooked on Phonics,'" he says. While many defended Cosby's statement—even the ugly manner in which he delivered it—it actually supports an inaccurate and prejudicial, although popular, point of view.

It's inaccurate because the landmark case that gave rise to the civil rights movement and that in effect ended sanctioned segregation was not a *deal*.[3] Granted, as a consequence of racialization, *Brown* may *function* as a deal. But it doesn't constitute one. There is no contract stipulating that blacks must behave or speak in a certain way in order to prove we deserve to benefit from the rights all blacks should have had long, long ago. But since laws, just like everything else, are raced in America, and since race still has a polarizing effect, *Brown* is stifled in its potential. This leads to comments like Cosby's that—perhaps inadvertently—justify the American racial apartheid that keeps blacks separated from whites and the corresponding American class apartheid that separates the $500-shoe-buying, Hooked-on-Phonics-denying folks from the middle- and upper-class blacks to whom Cosby delivered his speech.

In other words, segregation based on color may have been outlawed by *Brown,* but race (of which color was only one, albeit the prime, indicator) was not. The effect that *Brown* was intended to have, but has been prevented from having, would have voided race as a marker of difference that limits opportunities, especially educational ones, for black people. Instead, the full achievement of *Brown* is deferred—because the progress toward making race not matter stopped when the focus shifted from color to performance. Thus language, dialect, and accent must now be understood, at least in regard to black people, in the same way that skin color wrongly used to be (and in some cases still is), as outward signs of inward flaws, as verbal manifestations of inherent inferiority, as faults of character.

Of course, since one can't exist without the other, can't have racial behavior without first identifying a race, the shift from color to performance is at best inexact, and the aim imperfect, which makes it necessary to stress the differences between the main target (those who perform characteristic blackness) and those they look like (but who acceptably perform whiteness). As E. Patrick Johnson puts it in his discussion of the performance of the "'white-talking' black," that "person's authenticity is called into question by his or her 'own' based not solely on phenotype but also on the symbolic relationship between skin color and the performance of culturally inscribed language or dialect that refers back to an 'essential' blackness or whiteness" (2003, 7). Although he doesn't say it, Johnson implies that this "calling into question" can work both ways: not only can a black person's authentic racial identity be challenged by others because he "talks white," but a black person can also willfully *in*authenticate himself, can certainly attempt to disassociate himself from the race by deliberately performing what he knows others understand to be "white" ways or by expressing "white" views. This performative disidentification is a way of saying, "I'm not like other blacks." Therefore Cosby's words may be read as his attempt to use racial politics and conservative, even racist, views on black speech as the wedge that makes his blackness distinct—better—than that performed by the black lower class. It's another way of saying, point in the right direction: we may all be black, but we don't all act or sound like we are.

"It's standing on the corner. It can't speak English," Cosby continues to say as he objectifies and dehumanizes the black underclass. He claims, "I can't even talk the way these people talk," then mutilates a version of their speech: "Why you ain't where you is go, ra." Cosby says he heard a kid say that and was about to "blame" him "until [he] heard the mother talk" no differently. And, as if that wasn't bad enough, he says he then "heard the father talk" even worse. Needless to say, Cosby was disappointed—angry, even. "Everybody knows it's important to speak English except these knuckleheads," he says. "You can't be a doctor with that kind of crap coming out of your mouth."

It's no surprise that Cosby believes that BEV represents linguistic ineptitude and educational laziness. The linguist Rosina Lippi-Green points out that remarks like Cosby's may be misinformed, but they are not surprising. Too many view BEV as the prime indicator of "black resistance to a cultural mainstreaming process which is seen as the logical and reasonable cost of equality—and following from that, success." This is why, according to Lippi-Green "[BEV] evokes a kind of panic"—which Cosby personifies—because people want an accounting for why "desegregation has not done its job" (1997, 183). For those who believe as Cosby does, the blame lies not with the government and educators—who presumably have done their parts—but with lower-class blacks—who presumably have not. Many who don't speak BEV, and some who do, believe that giving up BEV is no loss at all compared with the benefits that the sacrifice is supposed to yield.

Thus it doesn't matter that more than thirty-five years of research on black and white language by linguists and educators persuasively argues that BEV is just as good as standard English and that the educational problems that blacks face do not stem from its use. It doesn't matter because BEV itself isn't the problem. Cosby wasn't disturbed, for instance, because he didn't understand the speakers he imagined. To him the use of BEV signals rejection of a "deal"—one that ensures the erasure of racism, or at least its reduction, on the basis of a quid pro quo. It's a way of saying that being black, and in turn racism, will become more irrelevant as lower-class blacks get better at performing their blackness in the right way. And, of course, the right way to be black, according to the profile in Cosby's diatribe, is to demonstrate middle-class values, conform to common gender norms within a family structure, be heterosexual, and, of course, speak standardized English.

The problem with this view is that it coerces people to pretend they belong to a socioeconomic class that rejects them, to conform their gender behaviors to mainstream expectations, to reorient their sexualities, and to exchange one racial way of speaking for another. Some of which many underclass people are willing to do and even more try to do, all, ironically, in order to make their blackness not matter when really it's all that does. For while the performance that Cosby advocates may help a few gain a little and even fewer gain a lot, the majority of us must face the fact that no matter how much we adjust, contort, or perform, performance will never make or unmake us black. To rephrase this impossibility as a question is to ask this: If black is something you're born with, something every black person embodies, how can some fail or succeed at being black or be considered to exhibit the right or wrong kind of blackness?

At first glance this question might seem to deflate the problem that I see in Cosby's comments. It might seem as if what Cosby counts as success is not exactly about reaching a certain racial rank, about achieving or refuting blackness, but rather about how language and behavior contribute to and represent a change in class status. This makes sense conceptually and is likely the reason *Brown* is viewed as a deal. After all, racial difference is fixed at birth and is impossible to change. Furthermore, based on my example, anyone who wants to change his race is deemed unstable or is told endlessly—although there is proof to the contrary—there is no such thing as performing race, no such thing as talking white or acting black. On the other hand, no one challenges the idea that you perform your class. This is because class difference, unlike racial difference, is only influenced by birth and therefore is considered unfixed and is frequently changed. This leads Cosby to believe that *Brown* has done its part; it paved the way for "the lower economic people" to change their class. Now they must get their acts together—literally—and do it.

The problem here is this: the difference between race and class does not apply in the same way for blacks as it does for whites (or for other people who are not black, such as Jewish people or Asian people). If it did, then changing class would not affect the question of blackness. But as it is, as Cosby's comments clearly show, the question of blackness, especially where language is concerned, is above all a question of class. The linguists Joshua A. Fishman and Erika Lueders-Salmon make this point plain when they explain that "in white eyes [and apparently also in the eyes of blacks,] Black English not only stamps one as black," as a sign of racial heritage and identity, "but [it also stamps one] as lower-class black," as proof of caste (1972, 79). Thus in a world where being lower class and being black are completely identified, the effort to stop being lower class must at the same time be understood as the effort to be white, or at least to stop being black, and, for boys, as the effort to stop being masculine.

This is why, as a boy who loved school and books, it felt to me in a psychological sense and looked to others in an expressive sense as if I were trying to be white. It also felt and looked as if I were not masculine enough. So I hammed up the white part because it helped to lessen a little the taunts about being a sissy. My peers experienced similar problems, but those who were able to perform different choices did so. They took being badasses over being fags. We each used name-calling and fistfights to get the other to act differently in order to validate ourselves. But this was not enough for me. I wanted to completely transcend this dilemma, which appeared to be distinctively black, so I longed to actually become white.

My experiences have often led me to think as Cosby does. Like him, I'm also tempted to blame lower-class blacks for my feelings, to use them as a scapegoat, a racial red herring. But trying to displace blame onto the masses who are still victimized by a society that pathologizes blackness will only make matters worse. Comments like Cosby's that don't take into account these complexities lead many "lower economic people" to view middle- and upper-class blacks suspiciously, as at once allies and antagonists. The friend who forwarded me a flurry of e-mails on the matter, for example, who knew I was writing this book and begged me to include a discussion of Cosby in it, said that Cosby's interests in the education of blacks and his philanthropy in that regard make him a friend. But my friend believes that Cosby's generosity gives him no right to have spoken so coarsely and uncritically, which makes him appear as a foe.

As a matter of fact, my friend thinks that Cosby is just as conflicted about race, class, and identity as I am and believes he should listen to a tape of his own speech patterns and those of his wife, Camille, whom my friend sees, despite her quite elegant public persona, as "the queen of Ebonics." I haven't had many opportunities to hear Camille Cosby speak, but my friend's disappointment and his intent to insult Cosby point up several facts about the conflict of racial authenticity: that Cosby's words exemplify the problem rather than help extinguish it; that as this problem continues, it gets more and more vicious; and that changing one's class status from lower class to middle class doesn't resolve the conflict. It hasn't for Cosby. And it certainly hasn't for me. In the next part I will discuss in more detail how detrimental views like Cosby's are to the educational success of black people and how those views keep blacks in conflict with one another.

2
SCHOOL

YOUR AVERAGE NIGGA

In the wake of calls by literacy educators in the early 1990s urging colleges and universities to hire more black writing teachers—"teachers," in Thomas Fox's words, who understand "the connections between literacy and African American culture" (1992, 301)—I was hired to teach part time at Columbia College, Chicago. I was the only black man teaching in a literacy program for underachieving first-year students, an unfortunate circumstance that worked in my favor in at least one respect: that year Columbia announced plans to increase its full-time minority faculty as part of its efforts to retain minority students, especially blacks. Of the ethnic minorities enrolled, blacks consistently had the highest dropout rate, with black men faring worst of all: 2 percent graduated after four years and only 4 percent after five. Consequently, the following year I was promoted to a full-time non-tenure-track position.

I was thrilled. But, evidently, some of the other (mostly white) hard-working part-timers were not. In particular, one teacher repeatedly questioned my credentials in that sneaky, fake, nonconfrontational way that Momma taught me to be suspicious of as a child when it comes from whites. "What year of the PhD program are you completing?" she asked. "What literacy theorists do you know? And, how much more do you want to teach literature instead of writing?" She punctuated each of my responses with "humph," followed closely by "How good for you." I would be laughing to myself, dying to say: "Lady, just be glad you're white."

I mean, sure, my race and gender helped me get hired. But the real task was to prevent those same factors from getting me fired. I was known, after all, for leaving jobs and losing jobs. "Good jobs!" Momma called them, as she shook her head, rolled her eyes, and complained that these were the teaching jobs she sent her "smart" son to college to get, not to quit. She asked the family and her friends to help her understand why I'd gotten myself run out of Mount Vernon High School in Mt. Vernon, Illinois, where some of my white students, from that nearly all-white working-class town, complained that the literature I taught was always pitting whites against blacks in ways that made them feel uncomfortable. And she wanted to know how it was that I couldn't manage to stay at the all-black Westinghouse High School on Chicago's West Side when I was just as black as they were. When I told her that I had been fagged and sissied out, that the black female principal had said, "Some of the students think you're not masculine enough. You got to change that. You got to act like a man," it puzzled Momma that I didn't just grin and bear it.

Momma thought I had finally found my niche the following year at Hoffman Estates High School in Hoffman Estates, Illinois, where she thought at least those white, liberal, middle-class suburbanites wouldn't think I was gay and probably wouldn't mind my teaching one or two black poems to white kids. But when I taught Countee Cullen's "Incident" and found myself looking white administrators squarely in the face, telling them with my eyes to kiss my ass and ready to tell them for real if they pushed me, Momma knew I wouldn't last long. She said that either I didn't want to work or I lacked what it took to keep a good a job, which required, we both began to realize, something other, or at least more, than an education.

So when I told her about working part time at Columbia, she said, "You should be glad that any place is taking a chance on you. Part time is better than no time: at least you can eat." And you can imagine her surprise when I told her about the promotion. She was happy but very cautious: "Don't go making them white folks feel uncomfortable by talking about race. It scares them, challenges their power—something."

But my response was the same. "Momma, my problems ain't just with white folks. And, even if they were, if I don't talk about race, how will my students ever know how their whiteness affects society before they leave their suburban neighborhoods and rural homes, go off to college or into the workforce, and carry on their lives as if slavery never happened, as if their fathers, maybe even their mothers, never call me nigger?"

It's not that I've ever been called a nigger, not to my face anyway. But I was trying to make the point—that just as Momma herself still believes some distant cousin or strange uncle in all-white families still refers to blacks as niggers when no blacks are around, that's no different from her calling whites crackers, peckerwoods, and honkies in private. In other words, race is just as important now as it ever was—even if both blacks and whites agree to pretend in public that it isn't. I told her that part of the race problem today, perhaps the biggest part, is due to our complicity in this pretense.

Momma, of course, was only exercising her hard-earned right to express concern, having successfully raised nine kids alone in the Governor Henry Horner Homes. Momma demanded nothing but excellence from her children—and got it. All nine of Momma's kids had graduated from high school at the very least, completed some college, and worked in professional jobs. None of the four boys nor any of the five girls was a teen parent. There are no drug addicts among us nor any who have spent time in jail (except me). This Momma image is not the common ghetto stereotype of the momma who struggles but ultimately fails to save her children from the tribulations of ghetto life. Nope, Momma beat the hell out the ghetto, and you better believe she was concerned about my success. She didn't want me to be like some other black men—many of those I grew up with—who were dead, in jail, selling drugs, working for minimum wage or not at all. But she said she didn't know how I would keep myself from ending up just like them, even with a PhD. And to be honest, I didn't either.

Neither of us understood at the time why an ambitious twenty-four-year-old with two master's degrees, who was working toward a

PhD, who had never done drugs or been in a gang, was nonetheless experiencing some of the problems that his education was supposed to help him avoid. Trying to figure out why I was having troubles doubled my purpose for teaching at Columbia. I was no longer aiming only to prove to Momma that I could keep a "good job"; I also wanted to understand why holding on to one was so difficult, particularly at a time when schools were vying for black male teachers. I knew that understanding this was inseparable from understanding what was expected of me as a writing teacher. It was clear that the hiring committee wanted what everyone who wants to hire a black male professor from the ghetto wants: for me to make the connections they couldn't with students they didn't fully understand and were therefore unable to assist as much as they wanted to. What wasn't so clear was how they wanted me to do it or if I even could.

However, the hiring committee and I both thought that if anyone could make helpful connections, someone like me should be able to. My class, gender, and racial characteristics mirrored those of the students they most wanted to save. And, as a college professor, I was an example of someone who had achieved an educational level to which it seems few black men from the ghetto aspire and that far fewer ever get close to. Of course, the hiring committee and I would have been mistaken to believe that my presence alone would dissolve excuses for why it couldn't be done, why other black males from the ghetto can't do well in school. In fact, the connections I make between the school and the ghetto lead me to argue that my shaky ghetto-to-middle-class trajectory supports less why black males *can* do well in school and more why they *don't*, even perhaps why they *can't*.

Further, it isn't, I've come to see, making connections between literacy and black culture that offers the best solutions to the problem of student retention (or for my own retention as a faculty member, for that matter). Instead, making those connections implicates the literacy classroom as a site that reproduces the retention problem it's designed to eliminate. This claim doesn't stem solely from my experiences as a former ghetto boy who has taught on all levels of education and in different cultural settings. I also base it on my observations of the cultural norms and practices of those settings, from having listened carefully to my teaching colleagues and from reflecting on the writing and self-presentation of my students, especially my black male students. In fact, it was one student in particular—I'll call him Cam—whose first essay for me provoked this chapter I'm writing for you. Cam attempted, as I'm doing here, to analyze the disconnection between literacy and black culture that hasn't yet been successfully reversed.

In his paper Cam writes that "your average nigga in the ghetto is given five words at birth" that he is fated to recite for the rest of his life. "These five words" constitute the ghetto newborn's lifelong defense plan and are guaranteed to "get him or her through every problem they face. These five words are 'I don't give a fuck!'"

Cam's words recalled for me the literacy scholar Kermit Campbell's study of papers by black inner-city male students who were natural code meshers, mixing popular street slang with academic discourse in their essays. Campbell's students' language habits didn't surprise him, nor did Cam's trouble me. Black vernacular discourse, after all, is an inseparable part of my native dialect. And Campbell's argument, that writing teachers should include an understanding of that dialect "in our writing pedagogies [in order to] affirm the social and cultural identities of many African American students," seems only logical and right to me (1997, 76).

Hence Cam's use of vernacular phrasing to construct his narrative thesis is not what disturbed me. What bothered me was his forceful but false assertion of indifference conveyed by those five words. They were words I had often used to mask the fear and pain that I experienced while growing up as a rather bookish boy with a high-pitched voice in the ghetto—a boy often teased and called sissy and fag, because I liked performing in school plays instead of playing sports. It didn't help that I had no "raunchy macho," couldn't develop that "special [pimp] walk," or that I was no good at the "distinctive handshakes and slang" that the early childhood education researcher Janice E. Hale-Benson describes as the "common manhood rites" for black boys (1986, 170). Because of this my gender performance was incompatible with what was required of black boys. So for psychological protection, I convinced myself that I didn't give a fuck about the ghetto and longed only to get out.

Therefore, when Momma nudged me to do well in school, I ran to it—straight into white cultural settings, where I was confused about whether my unexpected alienation was the result of being seen as a faggot or a nigger. I wondered what it was that white folks didn't like about me. Was it the way I walked or talked? Was it the color of my skin? Was I too angry? Too dangerous? Not dangerous enough? What? Saying "I don't give a fuck" was my only defense. And I wondered: What race wants me? This was a particularly tough question to answer since I imagined the whole world against me, as Cam obviously did too.

He continues: "Your average nigga is living in a hostile world that will chew you up and spit you out still whole." These words echo Momma's saying—"Ahma eat you up"—which she uttered right before she whipped her kids for disobeying her command. Being eaten up came to mean being punished by those demanding my compliance and fittingly figures the alienation I faced in the white schools I attended from high school on. The idiom also aptly characterizes the physical and verbal abuse I endured from my peers in the ghetto because they thought I identified with school too much. And Cam's (cum Momma's) phrase is also an expression of the intraracial conflict that exists between some middle-class blacks and their street-identified counterparts.

At least that was the case for Malcolm X, who exclaims, "He was trying to eat me up!" in describing a black college professor's reaction to him and his ideology. "He was ranting about what a 'divisive demagogue' and what a 'reverse racist' I was," X says about the professor. And in an effort to defend himself, X writes that he "was racking [his] head, to spear that fool"—and thought of a way to do it. "Do you know what white racists call black PhD's?" X sarcastically asked the professor, who responded: "'I believe that I happen not to be aware of that.'" So X "laid the word down on him, loud: 'Nigger!'" (1964, 284).[1]

Calling that professor a nigger was a way for X to neutralize the racial perspectives between him and the professor—perspectives that can be identified in X's street language and ideology and in the professor's contrasting beliefs and hyperliterate linguistic performance, what X calls "ultra proper talking." X wanted the professor to understand that blacks shouldn't have to talk or believe like the professor in order to be successful in school. For X the professor's speech and views not only represented identification with whites and wholesale assimilation into white culture but was also a way for some middle-class blacks to repudiate and distance themselves from other (ghetto) blacks. The racial politics that took place between X and that professor are emblematic of what happened between Cam and me. Only it wasn't Cam who called me a nigger to neutralize our differences. I called him one to amplify them.

Cam arrived in class on the first day about twenty minutes late, on what Momma used to call CPT (Colored People's Time). He was wearing baggy jeans, Nike sneakers, and a bright yellow Tommy Hilfiger jacket that hung low, and he was bobbing his head to music that pumped from headphones that he didn't remove until after he sat down in the very first seat to my left. That's when I smelled the scent of fresh marijuana, which I suspected he'd just smoked. And I thought, "Damn, why me?" And that's when I profiled him as a ghetto black man, like the ones I had grown up with and was trying to leave behind. That's when I thought of him—I'm sorry to say—as a nigger.

Obviously, the term didn't come to my mind as a way for me to identify with Cam, in the way that Campbell writes that blacks sometimes signify upon "the standard English pejorative label *niggers*," by replacing "*-ers*" with "the black vernacular *-az* to affirm" their identity and community "in the face of anyone or anything that poses a threat to blackness" (1997, 68). No, my thoughts about Cam came from the same racist view that prompts the vernacular term in the first place—a view of black male identity that Campbell says "society has defined or constructed . . . largely through negative images and exclusion." And, according to Campbell, "this negative imaging and exclusivity is nowhere more evident than [in the academy,] in the stance toward nonstandard language varieties" (71).

I wasn't intentionally being classist or racist when I profiled Cam negatively. I was responding to my fear and envy of his self-assured performance of black masculine identity—an identity that Phillip Brian Harper says personifies BEV (at least the popularized street version).[2] I felt endangered, not physically but racially. I felt as if my blackness had been jeopardized because, unlike Cam, I am not equally able to speak and personify BEV. Nor am I able to speak and embody the language I was called to teach—standard English, which, according to the linguist Rosina Lippi-Green, is an English vernacular based on the language norms of middle- and upper-middle-class white people (1997, 62).

I was worried that Cam would see me as a faggot and an Uncle Tom because, in the ghetto where I grew up, school was construed as the ultimate site of middle-class whiteness, likely because the mandated language variety for instruction was and still is a reified White English Vernacular. School was also viewed as a place best suited for girls, which, according to Hale-Benson, makes both black and white boys "feel [as if] they are flirting with homosexuality if they give in to the pressures of the school to exhibit behaviors they consider feminine" (1986, 66).[3] Because some boys see school as a site of effeminacy and school language (WEV) as a discourse for girls, white and black boys resist some forms of language instruction, which in turn causes them to fail literacy classes. But the difference between black boys and white boys is that black boys not only feel coerced to give up their masculinity if they do well in school, but they also feel forced to abandon their race—the ultimate impossibility. This feeling of racial and gender endangerment occurs not only in cases of black boys from the ghetto but is also experienced by black boys from middle-class communities like the one that the literacy scholar Erec Smith describes in his literacy narrative.[4]

Smith, who grew up in a middle-class, predominantly white community on the East Coast at the same time that I was growing up in the ghetto, attended an all-white elementary school, where, as he writes, "racial slurs were plenty and daily." Because of racism, Smith says that he felt "pressured into trivializing [BEV]." His white teachers and peers compelled him to give up his black dialect and identity. This induced in him "a need to escape" whiteness—and high school, where he would encounter more black people, gave him his chance to do it.

But when he "found fellow black freshmen, hung out [and] sat with them at lunch," Smith says he "quickly became just as much of an outcast, if not more of one, than I was amongst my former, predominantly white student body. To my African American peers, I was not really black. . . . The way I spoke gave them even more reason to come down on me." Smith's "proper speech," which he had embraced to fit in among his white peers in elementary school, made him appear to his black peers in high school to be, in Smith's words, "some sort of phony male" (2003, 436–37).

As with me, speaking WEV put Smith's blackness and masculinity at risk among other blacks. Citing William Labov's research "in male linguistic dominance," Smith writes: "It was discovered that in urban settings, standard pronunciation is associated with women more than men, making formal English a gender marker for women" (Smith 1999–2000, 436–37). Because of this, some black men risk subjecting themselves to homophobic antagonism if they speak and write standard English. This is an experience corroborated by Phillip Brian Harper. While analyzing the homophobic discourse that surrounded the AIDS diagnosis and death of the prominent black newscaster Max Robinson, Harper concludes, "Within some African-American communities the 'professional' or 'intellectual' black male inevitably endangers his status both as black and as male whenever he evidences a facility with Received Standard English—a facility upon which his very identity as a professional or an intellectual in the larger society is founded in the first place" (1996, 11). While Harper's point suggests that every black male who speaks WEV will undergo racial attacks on his masculinity, it may be more accurate to say that if those black males do not exhibit other behaviors considered to be masculine, such as displaying a pimp walk, playing sports, or engaging in sexual banter with females, they will inevitably endanger their black maleness.[5]

Not all black boys who are actually gay or effeminate speak WEV or are guaranteed to do well in school. Many blacks, regardless of sexual orientation or gender performance, choose to identify with their race over anything else (or are forced to do so). This leads me to believe that there is an understudied group of black boys who are gay and/or effeminate who don't do any better in school than their macho counterparts. I suspect that, to them, being black alone is enough to make school appear just as foreign as it does to some other black boys. I believe this because the choice that Smith and I were presented didn't seem to be the choice that it might seem on the surface: choosing between school or being black. We had to choose between being insufficiently masculine or insufficiently black.

Smith and I both experienced racial problems with whites in schools; because of the educational and middle-class advantages we would gain, and because we could maintain a sense of masculinity within a white context, we both chose to be insufficiently black. "I realized that I did not really want something as arbitrary as ethnicity" (Smith 1999–2000, 437), Smith declares in an attempt to reject race and ethnicity altogether in response to his experiences. But it wasn't race that I tried to reject. I just didn't want to be black. So I worked against developing ghetto masculine characteristics and learned to act and talk as a white man. It didn't take me long to discover that in the right environments, especially at school, the more I acted white, the more I seemed to succeed. In fact, becoming a high school English teacher and getting a PhD was a way for me to validate my anomalous black identity. It was also my way of claiming to be effeminate, not because I was or wanted to be gay but because I was smart. These reasons for becoming a teacher made my personal and professional conflicts even more pronounced, because I also quite sincerely wanted to reach back, as the saying goes, and help those in the ghetto. But when I was unsuccessful, I admittedly used my school success not only to excuse my gender and racial inadequacies but to avenge them. I wanted to vindicate myself for the way the ghetto had treated me. I used my facility with WEV and my apparent, though unstable, professional success as signs that I was better, as a way to confirm that my peers' poor prospects were their punishment for ostracizing me.

This is why I initially wanted to eat Cam up because he reminded me of what I loved but loathed even more. He reminded me of those students I'd taught in the ghetto, at Westinghouse High School, who speculated about my sexuality and called me a fag to my face, students who rarely went to college. But Cam was in college and in my classroom, no less. And I had mentally classified him as a nigger in order to stabilize my own non-"nigga" masculinity. And after I started to read his paper, I began to realize just how much my success hinged upon his failure. What had I really achieved if black males like Cam were coming to college and being successful? And would not my validating his use of the vernacular in order to affirm his black masculine identity demean my own?

To be sure, I was ready and willing to adhere to Campbell's pedagogical call to privilege BEV. But doing so for me meant being patronizing toward the ghetto, resisting the imposition of white standardization, and fetishizing black masculinity all at once. This odd admixture of racial politics left me feeling not only racially suspect but fearful of being continually on bad terms with all social and professional groups to which I belonged. I believed (and still do) that Campbell's argument privileging BEV is important for black linguistic inclusion because it makes space for more students like Cam to enter and do well in our classrooms. But I also know that it unavoidably reproduces the burden of racial performance—the burden of proving the kind of black person you are by how you act and talk—in a site where it was not as pronounced. The schools recognized neither burden nor problem, simply ostracizing students like Cam and embracing students like me. It was thought that one group belonged in the street and the other belonged in school. Now that we both are in school, I'm the one that is still forced to choose between being insufficiently black or insufficiently masculine. Campbell's pedagogy gives Cam the advantage as it takes it away from me (and perhaps from Campbell himself as well). If the academy privileges BEV, Cam can be both sufficiently black and sufficiently masculine in the ghetto and in school. And I'm left asking in school the questions that drove me out of the ghetto: Am I black enough? Am I man enough?

Thus privileging BEV simultaneously aggravates one problem even as it helps solve another. It helps integrate one type of black identity but ignores others. This is why, in his critique of Campbell's advice for teaching literacy to black students, the literacy scholar David G. Holmes is, like me, left wondering, "How do [literacy educators] avoid explicitly or implicitly applying [the] experiences [of some black men] to all other African Americans? How do we get some of our African American students to remain proud of the ways that Black Dialect can be used to construct their personal and cultural identity without deprecating other African Americans who don't bear the same relationship to it?" (1999, 60). And, "How do considerations of gender, class, or sexual orientation generate diverse interpretations of African American rhetoric?" (62).

These questions are apparently so frustrating that Holmes appeals to the status quo for answers and surrenders to linguistic discrimination just because it's the way things flow. "If Black dialect were the language of the marketplace," Holmes reasons, "then anyone would be rhetorically disadvantaged. But it isn't." As Holmes sees it, black students and their teachers must choose to value either BEV or WEV. As a teacher Holmes promotes the latter, saying, "if [a black student] cannot use the language of the marketplace [standard English], *for whatever reason*, then she is rhetorically disadvantaged" (59; emphasis added). To say this is to ignore well-known "linguistic facts of life," as the linguist Rosina Lippi-Green has called them (1997, 45). One of these facts, Lippi-Green writes, is that "at some time in adolescence, the ability to acquire language with the same ease as young children atrophies" (46). This means that a student's linguistic foundation is established in the first years of life and can rarely, if ever, be completely altered. This doesn't mean that people don't build upon their language skills. It means that later habits are always informed by the first ones. Teachers seem to want to eradicate BEV completely from black students' school language habits to ensure their success in speaking and writing. But BEV will remain a permanent part of their linguistic habits, even as they develop in language use. For Holmes to say that there is no satisfactory reason why some black students don't master standard English, given that BEV may be what they have learned first and it can't be completely erased, is so unreasonable that it's fair to say that he should have known better. This is especially the case since it has been thirty years since Geneva Smitherman argued against views like Holmes's, writing in her highly acclaimed book *Talkin' and Testifyin'* that language habits are "pretty firmly fixed by about age five or six" (1977, 199). And if those language habits are what we call BEV, then Holmes's "for whatever reason" blatantly disregards the natural linguistic skill associated with one group of people in favor of that associated with another.[6]

Like Holmes, I'm frustrated with the questions that arise from Campbell's pedagogy. But, unlike Holmes, my dissatisfaction doesn't lead me to endorse the status quo. That's what caused me to put Cam unconstructively into a racial profile. Instead, like Smith, I want to challenge "the concept of culture altogether" (Smith 1999–2000, 434), to investigate the problems that result from equating language with racial identity—because it's that equation that seems to transform the effort to teach black students to speak and write differently into the effort to alter who and what they believe they are. In a certain sense it converts the educational process into a form of assimilation and requires everyone—teacher and student both—either to accept or to refuse assimilation. This causes both students and teachers to suffer. Because many black students refuse assimilation, they are in effect refusing education, which in turn makes "many sensitive and well-meaning teachers," writes the famed educator Lisa Delpit, experience "a certain sense of powerlessness and paralysis" (1995, 166). These teachers think they've failed because their best strategies, including privileging BEV, don't seem to be effective. They feel handicapped because it seems nothing they do works. They don't know what to do, if to teach WEV is to be racist and to teach BEV is to inadequately educate their students. As a result, Delpit says, those who don't give up completely respond to this dilemma by choosing "wrongly, but for 'right' reasons not to educate black and poor children" (166). Rather than appear racist, they simply allow the students to keep using BEV, which won't give them access to what Delpit calls "the codes of power" (42).

I believe that Delpit is right, but her solution is wrong. She proposes a pedagogy of "linguistic performance" where teachers are supposed to teach students to be bidialectical or to code switch or, in other words, to use BEV at home and in black communities and WEV in school. The students in such a classroom, writes Delpit, can "take on the persona of some famous newscaster, keeping in character as they develop and read their news reports." Afterward, the teacher can center the discussion on "whether Walter Cronkite would have said [or written] it that way." It's unclear why Delpit believes this pedagogy is a way of "taking the focus [and stigma] off the child's speech" (54–55) and writing, when telling children to imitate a white newscaster is to tell them that their language and identities are not welcome in school.

What little black girl or boy (my example notwithstanding) is going to identify with an aging white man? How will they know, for instance, given the blurring of public and private spaces, when to talk and write like Cronkite and when to be themselves? In response to these questions, it seems that Delpit (like Holmes) appeals to the status quo. "We [teachers] can only provide them with the knowledge base and hope they will make appropriate choices," Delpit says (1995, 53–54), sounding no different from the powerless teachers she's trying to help. The problem that remains in this scenario, and that will continue to stifle the success of any strategy, is the problem of equating language with identity, which means that we must continue to exaggerate the differences not only between races but between languages in order to make the differences stick. Adhering to this practice, without critiquing it, has duped too many well-intentioned and bright scholars. The linguist Nancy Bonvillain, for instance, writes that black "children's linguistic problems [in school] . . . should be seen as resulting from their awareness of teachers' negative judgments and their ensuing rejection of teachers' demands" (1993, 174). Nevertheless, Bonvillain believes that code switching "is a reasonable compromise" (181) for educating black students.

But there's nothing reasonable about this strategy—not to me and certainly not to the noted literacy scholar Keith Gilyard. In his sociolinguistic self-study, *Voices of the Self,* Gilyard calls approaches like the one Delpit and Bonvillain encourage "enforced educational schizophrenia" (1991, 163)—because black students are forced to see themselves as embodying two different racial, linguistic, and cultural identities. Gilyard rightly recognizes the problem that code switching presents and supports the notion of pluralism. Pluralism is a more democratic sociolinguistic theory than code switching. It holds that all dialects and languages are equal in terms of structure, even if they are unequal in terms of prestige. "To the pluralist," Gilyard writes, "the crucial work involving language education is to develop a school system (and of course a society) in which language differences fail to have deleterious consequences for those whose language has been traditionally frowned upon" (1991, 73). But in practice pluralists have not yet attained their goals. Were they to do so, Gilyard predicts, "learning another dialect could not be a major problem [for black students]." In fact, it would be extremely difficult to *prevent* them from learning Standard English" (74).

The problem, of course, with Gilyard's pluralistic framework is that black students would still have to identify one language as theirs and another as something more standard. The association of standard English with a white racial profile wheels through the back door the code switching that pluralism kicks out the front. Pluralism can't be considered any different from code switching if one dialect is seen as right for school (standard English) and another right only at home. However, the difference Gilyard suggests is that both dialects would be acceptable in school. That would make them equal in terms of social prestige, and black students won't feel that learning standard English is an assault on their identity. The only way I see to achieve that equal prestige, however, is not by accepting pluralism but by undoing the erroneous assumption that the codes that compose BEV and the codes of WEV are so incompatible and unmixable because they're so radically different. It's almost as if the very people who would never accept the idea that black people and white people are radically different are happy to displace that acceptance onto a vision of white and black language.

Hence, if we continue to reduce standard English to one dialect and regard BEV as something completely different, not only won't we ever get to the crux of the problem of language discrimination but we will continue to generate fatuous remedies or not be able to offer any at all.[7] This is the fundamental problem with Smith's concept of race switching, which borrows from the sociolinguistic theory of code switching to form a pedagogical theory that allows students to represent more than one race in their writing. Although Smith believes that he's critiquing the concepts of culture and race, he is only challenging the idea that black students have to be only black—which leads him to suggest that they can belong to any race or to many races.

Because "ethnicity is not natural," Smith writes, "but a manmade construct," students should learn to develop multiple ways of being, "be as neotonal as the coyote of Native American trickster mythology, for '[h]aving no way, trickster can have many ways'" (Smith 1999–2000, 437–38).[8] I know the personal pain that Smith experienced in school, which is why I also understand his motivation for wanting to problematize the ideas of ethnicity and identity. We both realize that our world is committed to these ideas, but we differ in that he believes that "freedom" from them "is not having [one] way (read 'ethnicity') [but] adopting a particular way [read ethnicity or race] for every given situation" (Smith 1999–2000, 438). As a result he converts Delpit's code-switching pedagogy, what Gilyard calls "enforced educational schizophrenia," into a Sybil syndrome, where students must develop multiple personalities.

In the end Smith fails to make sound educational policy out of the strategies that he used to confront the hurt he experienced as a boy. "If one is to understand me," Smith writes, "or feel more comfortable around me if I comply to a certain ideology of being, so be it. There is no deception here. The only deception is to think that ethnicity is a rigid, natural, and vital truth" (Smith 1999–2000, 438). But why does making ethnicity less rigid count as a solution when the only effect of the kind of performing that Smith promotes will be to require that students demonstrate an amazing racial agility? This, of course, is a skill that Smith himself couldn't achieve, not in elementary school or in high school. So what makes him think that anybody else will be good at it? If black students can't or won't perform two racial identities, what makes Smith think they'll perform more? And why would they be better off if they could?

I'm not so pessimistic that I think that the problem is hopeless.[9] What I do think is that the problem is worse for those of us who experience the problem not only as teachers but as those who were born into the problem as black men. Because of this we have developed an acute sense of urgency for solutions. But not all the solutions work. In fact, some produce more problems than they help rectify. That's why, with all these questions and conflicting strategies about what is presently an insoluble problem, it's no wonder that Cam writes: "My 'friends' feel I am stupid for trying to get my money from books. I was told by one of these so-called friends that the only book I need is a pocket book, preferably stolen. He told me white America does not care how smart I am, as long as I'm black I'm not going no where."

The rhetorical distance that Cam places between himself and his peers (his "so-called friends") mirrors the academic gap that is growing between them. Cam's thoughts about his friends don't seem so much different from what I initially thought about him. He doesn't refer to his friends directly as niggers, but he doesn't need to. The implication is there. And when school precipitates this kind of division among people, it's no wonder there's black-on-black crime. I'm certainly not suggesting that snatching purses is the best way to resolve the educational conflicts that black students from the hood experience, but I do understand Cam's friend's disillusion. For Cam's friend school just can't offer a sufficient remedy for what he rightly sees as a problem much larger than the classroom. And it's not because the problem is too big and the classroom is too small and limited. Rather, his point, I believe, one I argue here, is that everything we do in the classroom—whether it involves devaluing BEV or valorizing it, allowing students to act white or act black—is a function of—in fact, a contribution to—the continuing racialization of our society. And as we continue to race society, we simultaneously class it, gender it, and sex it.

I believe this is also the root of why I couldn't keep a job—because I was no good at race switching, maintaining the racial identities and living up to the racial fantasies that people held about me and that I held about myself. Both the working-class and middle-class white high schools where I taught were confronting an influx of black students from big cities, like St. Louis (into Mt. Vernon) and from the inner city of Chicago (into Hoffman Estates). I was hired to show the black students how to be like me or, to be more exact, to show them how those who hired me thought I should have been. I was supposed to show them how not to be so black, that is, so ghetto black. I was supposed to teach WEV. But I was paralyzed. I didn't know whether to validate the black racial performances of the students or playa hate on them. What's more, I was less interested in helping black students and more interested in helping white kids to learn their way out of the racism that I saw in them. I wanted to draw attention to the language habits that white students thought were right and standard but were just colloquial white language, not really standard at all. But since other white teachers talked the way the students did and sometimes couldn't tell the difference between standard WEV and its nonstandard vernacular, just as I sometimes can't distinguish BEV from anything else, I was seen as incompetent.

I believe I had a much harder time than some other blacks because I was trying to reconcile some major societal issues while teaching in schools that were dedicated to reinforcing them. Some other blacks play it smarter, however. They choose. They negotiate for the sake of the job. And I understand that. After all, as Momma always says, "You gotta eat." Other blacks play the game by the rules, within the system, instead of bucking it. But I'm a black who says you only get more of what you already got if you don't buck it. Cam, however, believed the opposite. He knew that college would show him how to succeed in the world and positioned himself to learn what it had to teach. And he was in the prime position to learn. What?! With his race and masculinity intact there was only one thing left for him to realize:

> When I come to school, I see a whole generation of scholars getting ready to take on the new challenges of the world. Then I come home and I know there are no scholars here. The only scholars in the streets are dead. The only thing you are taught in the streets is pain, how to give it, how to take it, and, if you're lucky, how to avoid it. Since the only thing you really learn on the streets is pain, it is safe to assume the last test of the streets would be cheating death. If you win, you live to try again, if you lose, you die.
>
> This way of thinking has taken years of wrong people and wrong experiences. This way of thinking keeps our jails filled and our libraries empty. This way of thinking is killing off a breed that could take this world over if led right. Unfortunately, this way of thinking is all the ghetto has that is truly its own. This way of thinking kept me alive in those streets. This way of thinking has taken me to different levels in my life. But, most impor-

tant, this way of thinking separates those who play the game from those who stand on the sidelines and hope.

Cam may be ambivalent about the ghetto, seeing it on the one hand as having "taken [him] to different levels in [his] life" and on the other as "keep[ing] our jails filled and our libraries empty," but he's not ambivalent about his desire to get out of it. For him that's the whole point of school. What's interesting is that he has invested high hopes in his college education. And there's no ambivalence about it. College for him is where "a whole generation of scholars [is] getting ready to take on the new challenges of the world" in contrast to the ghetto, where scholars only end up dead.

I read this as Cam's critique of the idea that the problem for black students in our schools is the problem of black identity. The problem, as Cam sees it, is the problem of escaping poverty, and that problem (as he's helped me to see) is only made worse—in fact, insoluble—when we redescribe the tools for escaping poverty as tools for escaping identity or as ways to protect it. I'm not saying, as so many often do, that black students shouldn't see WEV as a threat to their identity. I think they have every right to, especially given who they are. They come to the classroom as black people rather than poor people, given that they and we are the products of a system of racialization that got started long before we were born and that looks like it will continue long after we're gone. In light of this, it can't make any more sense for me to say that we should ask students to ignore their identities than it does to ask them to ignore their poverty. They're bound together. I get that. But getting it doesn't make it right. And just because it's the way things are doesn't mean it's the way things have to be.

That's why I argue that the schools are a symptom of the problem and that what we do in them cannot function as a solution to the problem. I mean this especially for elementary and high schools, not for colleges per se. However, writing programs are institutionalized in colleges as service programs and function similar to high schools, a situation that presents a host of restrictions that must be overcome before those classrooms can really become sites of change. In short, as long as the only debate we can imagine ourselves having is the debate between BEV and WEV, it doesn't matter who wins, because no one wins—a few Cams will make it, a few Erec Smiths, and a few Keith Gilyards. But millions will continue to lose, particularly those who, as Cam writes, "stand on the sidelines and hope."

Postscript

I had all the students in that writing class that Cam took share their papers with the entire class—workshop fashion. Hands down, all the students thought Cam's papers were the best (probably because I publicly praised them and because Cam always bragged about his high grades). When I wanted to illustrate some strong rhetorical technique or flow of language, I asked Cam to read from his papers. He was always eager. Afterward, several white students wrote personal notes and e-mailed me, telling me that they couldn't write as fluently as Cam did. And although none of them thought of the way he or she wrote as white, some of them did say, "I can't write black." I explained to them that it wasn't that they couldn't write black. It was just that the social and cultural forces and school training that had influenced their rhetorical style were different from those that had shaped Cam's. I assured them that I understood WEV and would view their writing through that lens when I graded it. In the end, however, I was worried not only about whether Cam would pass his second semester writing course but also about my reputation as a writing teacher, and my job. Would I get to keep my good job if other teachers knew that I had given Cam an A?

After that class it was two years before I saw Cam again. I showed up unexpectedly in one of his classes, dressed in a blue business suit. It was a class on human sexuality, and Cam was sitting in the back, laughing along with the rest of the class at some joke the teacher had just told. I waved for him to come into the hall. He hesitated a moment. In the hall he told me that he thought I was a detective and that he was thinking to himself, "Damn, they gettin' bogus as hell, comin' to school to get you." We both laughed at that. After class we met for lunch. I gave him an early draft of this essay and asked if he would help me write about the problems I pose here. He took the paper; we exchanged numbers and e-mail addresses. A year went by—and nothing. No phone calls, no e-mails, and no responses to mine. I finished the essay alone, knowing full well that I've raised far more questions than I've answered. I'm sure that, had Cam and I written together, we could have provided much more insight but certainly not nearly enough.

As I was completing this chapter, six years after Cam and I met, I checked on his student status. He was a senior then. I hope he graduates.

CASUALTIES OF LITERACY

During my tenure at Columbia College, Chicago, I was asked to give a talk to fifty or sixty part-time writing teachers about the presence of vernacular in students' writing. I approached my discussion knowing that most teachers still support code switching, which I'm against. Given the egalitarian ethos and liberal politics that inform current literacy research and instruction, most teachers only parrot the expected response to the question of BEV—"Yes, respect it!" But this is often accompanied by an unspoken caveat: "As long as students use BEV with other blacks and WEV at school."

So I began my talk with the same argument and encouragement that I wish to advance here: Rebuff the ideology and pedagogy that seek to reduce so-called black dialect interference in speech and writing. Focus instead on the inextricable stylistic and rhetorical value of BEV, for as the anthropologist Signithia Fordham (referencing Felicia Lee [1994]) makes clear, "black discourse style increases rather than diminishes the longer Black students are in school" (1999, 287).

Since BEV ain't goin' nowhere, it only makes sense that we should allow students to combine it with the discourse we're required to teach, a strategy that I call code meshing. Accepting code meshing would mean abandoning the Ebonics approach or, rather, what should be called the Ebonics concession, where students are either instructed in BEV and then required to translate it into standard English or are given a choice of using vernacular in creative assignments but not in formal papers. I promote a thorough, seamless mixture of BEV and WEV that leads to more natural, less artificial, well-expressed prose. The benefits of code meshing extend beyond producing better papers. I believe it will help teachers avoid imposing the harmful effects of American racialization on students, which happens when we view their linguistic habits as subliterate, fundamentally incompatible with what's considered standard.

My position echoes arguments of years ago that advocate against code switching and that, fortunately, are being revived in current research on education and writing. Take, for instance, Gerald Graff's belief that the rigidity that accompanies most instruction in standard English does a disservice to all students, particularly blacks. For Graff (2003) common speech and street smarts are useful to education in general and academic writing in particular and not just as a means to an end, as if BEV were merely a bridge to be crossed to get to standard English. He illustrates his claim in an analysis of the sociolinguist William Labov's interview with Larry, a black teenager.[1] For Graff, Larry's working-class vernacular response—"He'd be white, man"—to Labov's question of God's race is more forceful than what many white middle-class speakers might utter. Further, Graff finds Larry's reply to Labov's follow-up question—Why?—to be clear and articulate. Larry responds: "Why? I'll tell you why. 'Cause the average whitey out here got everything, you dig? And the nigger ain't got shit, y'know? Y'understan'? So—um—for—in order for that to happen, you know it ain't no black God that's doin' that bullshit" (quoted in Graff, 2003, 37). According to Graff, Larry's "powerful, cogent, and interesting" (37) expression suggests that code meshing, a way of speaking and writing that combines BEV with formal English "seems preferable to code switching," which prevents these English varieties from intermingling. In short, as Graff puts it, "linguistic integration is preferable to segregation" (27). And, as I asked in the conclusion to my speech at that teachers' meeting, shouldn't it be?

It didn't take long for Diane to answer no. She was the only other black teacher in the room. I had noticed that she had sat unusually stiff backed and stone faced during my presentation. Her unemotional expression surprised me, since we had been generally friendly toward one another the few times we'd met before. As she spoke, however, it became evident that she had been masking her fuming discontent.

"I too want to help black college students write better," she stood and said, "because the ones who come to intern at the advertising company where I am an account executive can't write their way out of a paper bag." This, Diane declared, is what prompted her to begin teaching writing when she could spare the time.

Everyone knew that, despite our both being black, Diane was espousing a different position from mine on how the politics of race should inform the way we teach writing. This difference led her to contend that my advocacy for "code meshing sells black students short; it suggests they can't master the standard dialect." She said it would impair their ability to demonstrate the kind of rigorous, academic writing she would expect, regardless of race.

I stood in front of the room, trying unsuccessfully to don the same stony disposition that Diane had displayed earlier. I managed to hear Diane without getting too hot, that is, until she announced: "I'm black too. And I'm quite familiar with the codes of BEV. I know them better than anyone here might suspect. But I also know when and where to use them. No business out there is going to allow students or me to bring those codes to work, so we shouldn't allow them in here." Then she added, "I don't make the rules. I just follow them. I want to teach my students how to do so as well."

With that, Diane almost stopped, but she received such loud applause that she rose again. This time, speaking directly to me, she said somewhat sympathetically: "Look, you're a nice guy. I know this is personal for you, and I know you mean well, but far be it from me or you or anyone of us here to limit the chances for success of any minority student, especially underprivileged blacks, who need to learn the language of public communication in order to make it in this world."

She finished her rant with an example of someone whom she thought best showed why we shouldn't code mesh—me! "Look at you," she pointed, "a well-dressed, well-rehearsed, polished, articulate, black male college professor—how'd you get here? Students should have the same opportunity to become English professors. But they won't if we let them continue to do ghetto literacy."

Although I had anticipated this juxtaposition of ghetto black versus middle-class black and had come prepared to discuss its role in aggravating the gap between the classes, my anger got the best of me; I was all set to go ghettomatic and eat Diane up. I was set to signify on the fact that she wore a fur coat in early November before it seemed necessary, a symbol for me of middle-class pretension. I was also going to point out her ultraproper racial speech performance: the way she always pronounced *the* with a formal sounding long *e*, even when it wasn't exactly appropriate. I placed this speech habit within the same realm as Momma's (and my own) "Talkin' Proper." That is, there are times when Momma deliberately affects both intonation and speech patterns commonly associated with white people when she thinks someone white, or at least important, is on the phone. These were idiosyncrasies of Diane's that flared up during our discussion as traits to knock. But I kept quiet because Momma had taught me better. "If you ain't gone say nothing good 'bout a person, go on 'head 'bout your business," she'd say, putting a black spin on the old saying.

Although I haven't always followed Momma's advice, the applause that Diane received suggested I should. Instead of getting the teachers to interrogate our instructional practices and the unconscious beliefs that inform them, I landed in the hot seat. Diane had successfully deflected attention from the issues and onto the image of the transformed ghetto boy. Apparently, this figure was enough to get teachers to believe that whatever it took to sculpt my class profile into a manicured prototype, whatever pains I underwent to become the eloquent black male teacher giving a talk to a mostly white audience, and whatever struggles I might still face are par for the course—necessary. According to Diane, I personify a conservative brand of literacy instruction that I should promote, not denounce.

I denounce Diane's belief because it surrenders to prejudice. She doesn't deny that prejudice exists, but she wants students to dodge its consequences by not using BEV. Further, she is satisfied with a financial solution. As I see it, the problem of language prejudice is primarily an ethical issue. Economic consequences are certainly at stake. But our current class structure is established on a set of racist beliefs that need to be exposed and changed. This is why I don't believe that the black masses should do what a few so-called successes have been able to do. I believe the few are exceptions, which doesn't necessarily mean they're exceptional. How the masses are treated, their fate, paints the real picture. Dealing with the circumstances that prevent their success, rather than trying to package mine, is the real task we should take up.

Since so many teachers agree with Diane, I want to use this chapter to expand my argument, beginning with a similar situation that prompted the literacy scholar and critic Victor Villanueva to write "Whose Voice Is It Anyway?" (1987). The issues that came up during my interactions with Diane are also concerns of Villanueva's. His take on the journalist and author Richard Rodriguez underscores points that I had in mind at the meeting and want to pursue here.

Villanueva recalls listening to Rodriguez's guest lecture to the National Council of Teachers of English (NCTE) in which Rodriguez "spoke of how he came to be an articulate speaker of this standard dialect" (1987, 17). Villanueva says the English teachers present for the speech sat at rapt attention. They saw their work implicated in Rodriguez's success, a connection he makes himself in his acclaimed memoir *Hunger of Memory*. Rodriguez writes that he went to "a school where all of [his] classmates were white and many were the children of doctors, lawyers, and business executives." In stark contrast he was "a bilingual child," "'socially disadvantaged,' the son of working class parents, both Mexican immigrants," and "able to understand [only] fifty stray English words" (1982, 11, 12). Despite these setbacks, he grew up to get his PhD in English and become an influential writer and a sought-after speaker—all because, as he says, "My teachers were unsentimental about their responsibility. What they understood was that I needed to speak public English" (19).

Rodriguez uses his experiences in school to justify a polemic about language and literacy education. Most directly, he believes that bilingual education is a mistake, and by extension he also believes "black English [is] inappropriate in classrooms" (33). He describes bilingual education as "a program that seeks to permit non-English-speaking children (many from the lower class) to use their 'family language' as the language of school." In response to such a proposal, Rodriguez says, "[I] am forced to say no" (11–12). But his no comes at a personal and cultural expense. He writes about how, as a result of his acquired English-language education, he became estranged from his family, particularly his father, and how his Spanish heritage became like a foreign culture. All this was agonizing, he says, but worth it to achieve his goals.

Rodriguez uttered these sentiments in his lecture at the NCTE conference, where, according to Villanueva, "he was impressive," had "a quiet eloquence," and was a match for "Olivier's *Hamlet*." All this overwhelmed the teachers, who gave Rodriguez what Villanueva describes as "an enthusiastic" yet "uncritical acceptance, marked by a long, loud standing ovation." Villanueva says he "was surprised because [Rodriguez] had blurred distinctions between language and culture, between his experiences and those more typical of the minority in America, between the history of the immigrant and that of the minority, in a way that [Villanueva] had thought would raise" not "the audience to its feet" but "more than a few eyebrows" (1987, 17). The difference between the minority and the immigrant, which Rodriguez blurred, was of concern to Villanueva because some immigrants are eager to assimilate and often have opportunities to do so, whereas minorities are often disallowed complete assimilation even when they try. According to Villanueva, to conflate these two sets of experiences is not only illogical but erroneous. In the end, Villanueva says, "Rodriguez told the teachers to continue to be sensitive but to forget about doing anything special" (17). Rodriguez presented himself as the product of the teachers' traditional best practices; he saw himself as more than the proof—he was the pudding itself.

Rodriguez's claim is similar to the rhetorical move that Diane made and the advice she gave the teachers at our meeting—using me as the example. Like Diane, Rodriguez believes, according to Villanueva, that "the old ways may be painful, but they are truly best." Also like Diane, Rodriguez thinks "linguistic assimilation is like alchemy, initially destructive perhaps but magical, creating something new and greater than what was." From this both Diane and Rodriguez admonish teachers to "do as [they] have always done" (Villanueva 1987, 17). This advice sounds as wrong to Villanueva as Diane's sounds wrong to me. As Villanueva writes, "One person's experiences must remain one person's, applicable to many others, perhaps, but not all others" (21).

The problem that Villanueva has with Rodriguez, and that I have with Diane, is not only about the application of monolithic solutions to all students but about translating bad solutions into universal ones. When Villanueva thinks "of an eighty per cent dropout rate among Puerto Ricans in Boston, of Mexicans in the Rio Grande Valley where the dropout rate exceeds seventy per cent"; when he thinks "of places where English and the education system do not address the majority—Spanish speakers for whom menial labor has been the tradition and is apparently the future," he "must ask how *not* bilingual education in such situations" (1987, 21). Likewise, when I think of the rampant failure among black students, especially at Columbia College, Chicago, where more than 90 percent don't make it to graduation, I also ask how *not* code meshing.

But just as so many teachers find all kinds of reasons not to support bilingual education, so too many writing teachers find all kinds of excuses not to back code meshing. Some flat-out disregard the words of critics like Keith Gilyard, who grew up code switching. He doesn't believe that other black students should undergo the same trials he underwent to get to where he is. In fact, he too criticizes Rodriguez's "self-annihilation" and "cultural suicide" (1991, 160–61), which Gilyard says aren't so much necessary evils for minorities as they are "merely evil" (Gilyard 1997, 327). This is especially the case, Gilyard thinks, when teachers translate Rodriguez's "appraisal of his pain into pedagogy" (Gilyard 1991, 161).

Others who oppose code meshing are heartened by the historical and popular bias against BEV. The writing theorist Lynn Z. Bloom, for instance, promotes her own fatalistic resignation to linguistic segregation. In her essay "Freshman Composition as Middle Class Enterprise," she says we shouldn't privilege BEV because "there is little evidence that American culture at large, despite increasingly multicultural classrooms, will grant equal opportunity for [BEV] to be valued on par with Standard English" (1996, 671). Bloom camouflages the linguistic prejudice she supports with a pseudoegalitarian approach. Teachers should not penalize students for using vernacular "while they are also learning the dominant standard," she writes. Yet she requires those same students to recognize the "innumerable *other contexts* where alternative dialects are appropriate" (671; emphasis added). This is the code-switching approach I argue against and that Villanueva also finds unfavorable. "Limiting the student's language to the playground and home," he writes, "still speaks of who's right and who's wrong, who holds the power" (1987, 21). But, like Diane, Bloom is adamant: "Like it or not," she says, "we are a nation of Standard English" (1996, 670). My response to Bloom is the same one that Villanueva gives to the teachers who embraced Rodriguez: "I would rather we left speaking dialects relatively alone" (1987, 21).

To be clear, it's more than the notion of standard English that I'm against. It's the methods that teachers use to get students of color to use it—methods that ultimately make many refuse it. Also problematic is the vague and limited scope of codes used to define standard English—a definition that determines more what standard English *is not* than what it is. Following from that is a serious question about whose political-economic interests are best served by restricting the meaning of what's standard. The all-too-common response from teachers to such concerns leads Villanueva to observe: "When it comes to the nonstandard speaker, we are torn between the findings of the linguists and the demands of the marketplace" (1987, 21).

My response, which admittedly may be easier said than done, is that teachers should be more, not less, critical of the "marketplace." We should prepare students for societal change, not merely to fit in. Our job should be educating students, not refashioning them into what we imagine the "marketplace" demands they should be. We should be encouraged by research that gives BEV parity with WEV— and that values both in school, in student papers, and in their speech. We should struggle for both to be thoroughly mixed together in the marketplace. If we don't, we follow Diane and Bloom and kowtow to phony social and political prescriptions for moving up the American class structure.

I acknowledge that the promise of upward socioeconomic mobility is seductive. But, if truth be told, the promise coming from education today is a fantasy. While the educational guidelines for navigating the American class structure pay lip service to providing opportunities for all, the real function of those guidelines is to keep most of those born at the top on top. In light of this, Diane and Bloom are wrong to urge that we teach WEV just so BEV speakers may play climb-the-socioeconomic-ladder when everybody knows the game is rigged and the rungs are weak. When blacks fall and lose—as many inevitably will—they become brick and mortar in the foundation that sustains the current American class structure. The linguist Wayne O'Neil puts the point this way: "The enterprise of making lower-class speakers over into middle-class speakers is simply a piece of the educational emptiness that helps maintain the present distribution of power in society. For wasting time there, on a thing that is bound to fail, serves to render school children skilled enough to be exploited but finally uneducated, used to failure, and alienated enough not to oppose exploitation" (1973, 190).

According to O'Neil, asking lower-class black students to bifurcate their linguistic abilities does not for the most part increase their chances to become middle class. In actuality, this practice does more harm than good and promotes failure rather than success. It unrealistically expects those who grow up speaking a language variety to drop it. Youngsters, especially college students, are smart enough to recognize this. Where they once saw education as a beacon of hope, after years of experience with linguistic tyranny, they lose hope.

Take Mica, for example. In "Failure: The Student's or the Assessment's?" Kay Harley and Sally I. Cannon describe Mica as a nineteen-year-old, new single mother. She is so eager to be in school that she writes: "Being in an college english class I felt I was final going to learn something about this word call english" (1996, 70). Harley and Cannon write about Mica because, despite her enthusiasm, she failed their writing course, while their white students passed. What were Mica's problems? Her teachers' list is long: her "direct discourse was often unmarked"; her "sentences are sometimes fragmented or fused"; the "missing tense markers, particularly 'd' or 'ed,' and copula ('to be') deletions reflect Black English Vernacular (BEV)"; and "she was unable or refused to squelch the personal" (1996, 74–75).

Reflecting on how "Mica's paper challenged [their] habitual ways of assessing writing," Mica's teachers wondered whether her "writing might have a rightful place in a freshman writing course and in academic discourse more generally" (1996, 75). To answer this question they reread Mica's writing through the black verbal tradition. From this code-meshing perspective Harley and Cannon found reasons to validate Mica's writing and sing her praises: "Mica's writing does render the immediacy of her experience. . . . It is filled with strong details. . . . [Its] rich rhythm gives the piece poignancy and power" (75). They even compare Mica's writing to the work of white female academics, like that of Jane Tompkins, "who call upon their personal experience to enrich and organize their understanding of professional concepts. If Tompkins can do it," the teachers ask, "Why not Mica?" (81).

Thus after a medley of compliments mixed with censure—"read as a whole, Mica's papers have a surprising unity," but "all fail to clearly and explicitly link example to generalization"—Mica's teachers acknowledge their "need to understand [her] errors, not as deficits, but as attempts at appropriating the discourses of other communities" (1996, 84). However, in the way these matters so often go, their analysis and subsequent confession do nothing for Mica. The teachers ultimately end where they begin. "We have no clear answer to the question. . . . Was the failure Mica's or that of our assessment procedure?" (85). But they do know one thing for certain. "Would we pass Mica's portfolio today?" They answer emphatically, unequivocally, no (85).

It's alarming that Harley and Cannon offer no word, no account, nothing to explain why they wouldn't pass Mica after reassessing her work. What difference would their reframing their assessments and attitudes have for students like Mica later on, in other classes? What would motivate teachers to take BEV into account when assessing their black students, when such reconsideration constitutes a challenge for teachers but ultimately has no positive effect on students?

To be fair, any teacher who confronts a student like Mica should experience some degree of conflict while endeavoring to meet the project of education, an enterprise that, as Bloom writes, sometimes mandates that teachers "punish lower-class students for not being, well, more middle-class" (1996, 655). This is important to note because the difference between lower-class white students and lower-class black students in literacy classrooms is difficult to measure without accounting for the role of race. For poor white kids, learning how to write is part of a process that involves learning how to escape their social class. While passing a college English course doesn't guarantee them middle-class status, it at least propels them toward that status while keeping their fundamental racial identity intact. For poor black kids, learning how to write involves not only escaping their class but repudiating the language that bespeaks their race, which feels not only as if they're acquiring a new class status (which could be a good thing) but also as if they must lose their race in the process.

Many well-intentioned, liberal teachers like Harley and Cannon, who observe this difference among whites and blacks but don't understand it, begin to second-guess themselves when they pass their white students and fail their black ones. Convinced of their integrity, they confirm they're not racists. But when the problem remains, they must locate it someplace. So first they displace it onto their assessment practices—as if such practices are divorced from their own ideology—and then onto students. Thus the class background of black students or their culture is viewed as the source of the problem when it really isn't. Then what is?

Bloom's essay provides a clue. She writes that "nineteenth- and twentieth-century pedagogical practices and [literacy] textbooks," which themselves derived from "eighteenth and early nineteenth-century" ideologies of rhetoric and social class, are direct sources for the "folkways" that she says students must "absorb" in modern-day introductory college writing courses (1996, 656). That being the case, then Gavin Jones's insightful essay "Whose Line Is It Anyway? W. E. B. Du Bois and the Language of the Color-Line" helps us understand how those "folkways" apply to blacks.

Jones writes that "the notion of the 'Veil'"—Du Bois's metaphor for the invisible shawl that separated blacks from whites—"was just as important to discussions of linguistic division as it was to social segregation" (1997, 25). This means that Jim Crow laws were instituted just as much to outlaw integrated language habits as they were to outlaw integrated race relations. This linguistic segregation was the outcome of nineteenth-century language debates. At stake was whether to separate black language from white language or consider them versions of the same.

This question arose because "accounts of the Southern dialect of American English before the Civil War . . . noted that Southern Whites from all class backgrounds learned the grammar and pronunciation of black English and retained the habit throughout their lives, becoming in effect 'bidialectical'" (G. Jones 1997, 21). But after the Civil War, as Gavin Jones notes, "the comparative tolerance of black English by the wealthy whites before the Civil War, which led to the observation that the color-line had broken down in Southern speech, was destroyed by the new situation, in which poor whites and blacks were thrown into competition, and in which the tracing of white language to black influence was felt as a deep insult" (23). Thus the "debate over language," Jones writes, "revolved around white fear that the cultural fabric of the South may have been produced by the weaving together of two cultural strands (broadly speaking, the Anglo-American and the African-American) into a new, hybrid mode" (24).

Efforts to expunge BEV from WEV led to overstated depictions of the differences between the two. Referencing William Cecil Elam's essay "Lingo in Literature" (1895), Gavin Jones writes that "while in actual life black speech and white speech were virtually identical, when they were depicted in literature black speech was exaggerated in its 'lingual barbarisms' while white speech was 'revised according to Noah Webster and Lindley Murray,'" which amounted to "an act of discrimination" (1997, 23). In short, white speech was represented in print as correct, even though in practice it was just as incorrect as black dialect when compared with grammar books and dictionaries.

The logic that supported this linguistic discrimination hinged on what Jones calls a paradox, "the paradox that black language was essentially different from, yet entirely familiar to white language; that it was separate from white language without being unnervingly 'other'" (1997, 24). As a result black speech took on an exaggerated characterization, becoming a grotesque caricature that could be used as evidence of black inferiority. White speech was also exaggerated but became virtuous and beatific. Exaggerated black speech was used as "sufficient cause for racial segregation." Exaggerated white speech became what blacks must learn to justify their right to integration, to equality (G. Jones 1997, 25). Thus, as Signithia Fordham writes (referencing Grace Sims Holt), "once Black Americans were freed from official enslavement, language became the major vehicle for perpetuating the legitimation of subsequent stages of oppression" (1999, 278).

In other words, despite the undoing of legal racial discrimination in 1954 with the *Brown* decision, language bigotry remains. This bigotry was expressed, according to Henry Louis Gates Jr., in the hopeful "predictions during the civil rights era that [BEV] would soon be a necessary casualty of school desegregation" (1988, xix). It was thought that interaction between blacks and whites would erase BEV. But, as Gates observes, "[BEV] has not, however, disappeared. . . . The black vernacular has assumed the singular role of the black person's ultimate sign of difference, a blackness of the tongue" (xix). Efforts to make BEV "a necessary casualty" also remain. These efforts result not in the erasure of the language—or even in its reduction—but in too many human casualties, students who fail or who have become jaded by education.

We know, then, that mid- to late nineteenth-century American ideologies of class and literacy were prejudiced against black speech. We should recognize that we accede to this prejudice when we apply those ideologies to the instruction of blacks or, for that matter, to white students. On the matter of literacy and white students, scholars have long observed, particularly in the famous document "Students' Right to Their Own Language" (1974), that Americans tend to believe that whites speak and write better than blacks when they really don't. Consequently, whites are often led to believe their speech is standard when really it's not. This state of affairs is being exposed because of its negative consequences for literacy practices in the workplace.[2]

It's not my intent to be too critical of teachers who genuinely want to do right by black students. I'm more critical of the prevailing ideologies of our educational system, which preclude all teachers from doing their best work with students. A. Suresh Canagarajah is the particular example I have in mind. He's a remarkably committed educator. Few can fill his big shoes when it comes to challenging linguistic and racial oppression, both nationally and internationally. Yet, like so many of us, he's required to participate in and perpetuate the practices he fights against. In his 1997 essay, "Safe Houses in the Contact Zone," he argues that teachers should promote "safe houses" for black students in our classrooms. For him safe houses are opportunities for black students to develop confidence in their educational abilities by associating with one another and using BEV with each other without penalty.

He's building on the critic Mary Louise Pratt's notion, which she first expressed in a 1990 speech and published the next year, that "safe houses" are necessary "social and intellectual spaces where groups can constitute themselves as horizontal, homogeneous, sovereign communities with high degrees of trust, shared understandings, temporary protection from legacies of oppression" (1999, 595). These spaces are essential because classrooms are contact zones, "social spaces," according to Pratt, "where cultures meet, clash, and grapple with each other, often in contexts of highly asymmetrical relations of power, such as colonialism, slavery" (584). In a way, safe houses can be likened to rooms where a li'l bro receives encouragement, is heartened by his peers, who also help him develop strategies to survive his ongoing battle with Big Brother.

Safe houses, according to Canagarajah, provide at least two big benefits to black students: They allow students to develop a sense of racial security in a zone that opposes them. And, in terms of literacy, students can learn and practice what Pratt calls "the literate arts (think here of linguistic martial arts) of the contact zone," which will help them to engage in "critique, collaboration, bilingualism, mediation, parody, denunciation, imaginary dialogue, [and] vernacular expression," among other techniques (1999, 590). These arts are expressed in a long letter (in the form of a book) that Pratt says an Andean li'l bro, Felipe Guaman Poma de Ayala, wrote to Big Brother, in this case, King Philip III of Spain, "after the fall of the Inca empire to Spain." Guaman Poma's letter, she says, was "written in two languages," "in a mixture of Quecha and ungrammatical, expressive Spanish" (1999, 584–85).

That Quecha, which apparently was Guaman Poma's native language, "was not thought of as a written language" and those who used it were considered illiterate, is important in this context. It reflects what we think about BEV and arguments against its use. It also reflects the consequences of restricting its use. Because of his writing style and dominant perceptions of it, not only in Spain but also later in America, it took 350 years for Guaman Poma's letter to be recognized as the "extraordinary intellectual tour de force that it was" (Pratt 1999, 584). Texts like Guaman Poma's, writes Pratt, "often constitute a marginalized group's point of entry into the dominant circuits of print culture" (586). If we recall Mica and her teachers' perceptions of her writing, we see the direct application. The writing classroom is a "dominant circuit of print culture," and students from oppressed groups often write papers in two languages that could be just as brilliant as Guaman Poma's letter. But black students' writing is often subject to the same highly indeterminate fate as Guaman Poma's text. Their writing is not given the reading it deserves at the time when a fair reading could do the most good. This is where Canagarajah's course reenters.

The class that Canagarajah describes was part of a university program designed to "induct [minority] students gradually into the 'academic culture' in order to improve their retention rate" (1997, 174). Ten black students took the course, and he observed all of them using a "range of discourses" in a safe house that they constructed while participating in an electronic discussion group that their teacher set up. He describes their use of BEV in the safe house as dazzling. As a result "the attempts [that black students] make to construct hybrid texts is immensely useful" to writing instruction, he says (191). He further suggests that teachers should assure students "that their vernacular discourses are valued academically, and that they don't have to be practiced in secret" (193). This is a version of the code-meshing argument that I make.

The problem I want to point out is this: while Canagarajah's recognition of the implicit value of BEV is commendable, the fact is, judging from the evidence he provides, his students did practice their vernacular "in secret." He required his black students to dissect their language habits, to separate BEV from WEV. He writes: "The approach I adopted for my course called for a sensitivity to the vernacular discourses and communicative conventions that minority students bring to the classroom, while enabling them to gradually cross discourse boundaries and get acquainted with the academic conventions" (1997, 175). His approach seems promising, but in the next sentences we learn what this "sensitivity to their vernacular" means in relation to "academic conventions": "Although students are encouraged to employ their vernacular discourses *in their own community (and possibly in informal contexts in the academy)*, they are expected to master academic discourse to communicate successfully in college" (175; emphasis added). This is the separate-but-equal approach that is so standard, an approach that the linguist Elaine Richardson says creates detrimental circumstances for black students. "Once students realize that writing their words is not acceptable [in the larger university context]," she writes, "stereotype threat sets in and they get caught between two worlds, writing something that is neither [BEV] nor academic English but something else" (2004, 163).

This "something else" is exactly what Canagarajah's students produced. "In comparison to the verbal disputes conducted [among themselves]," he writes, the essays they wrote for him "lacked conviction and force" (1997, 186). While analyzing this writing failure in one student essay, he says he found the same failure in most. "Several other students failed to sustain the debate or rebut opposing views forcefully," he writes, "as they did in the person-centered arguments [among themselves]" (187). Canagarajah's approach set off the very disparity he observes. What's worse, his approach may have contributed to his students' accusing one of their peers of "acting white" because she received a better grade than they did on one of her essays (178). This accusation is a fitting description of the circumstances that Canagarajah stipulated. He required students to exclude BEV from their papers, consequently contradicting his own avowed wish to respect it. So, because the student accused of "acting white" had demonstrated traditional black speech and behaviors with her peers, her writing performance was perceived as her attempt to act white, a show of her mastery of white language patterns.

Actually, it's hard to tell what linguistic approach the student accused of "acting white" uses because Canagarajah doesn't provide any excerpts from her paper. But it's not hard to argue that "acting white," at least in this case, is not an effect of a black inferiority complex or of blacks' wrongly thinking that school is only for whites. Instead, it's an effect of racialization, where behaviors considered to be white, like academic prose, are presented as superior by teachers because universities stipulate it. Even though I believe that Canagarajah ultimately provides good suggestions for teaching literacy to black students, I also believe his approach contributed to his students' viewing each other suspiciously—in racially segregated terms. It would seem that since Canagarajah framed his course by using the work of Pratt, which provides an example of a code-meshed text and the literate arts that produced it, he should have started where he ended. Instead, he first imposes code switching, then argues for code meshing. Some may say to this situation what I imagine some say about the severely delayed but ultimate arrival of Guaman Poma's letter: "It's better late than never."

In the case of many black students, however, late *is* never. This is why I argue for code meshing. If the modern-day introductory writing classroom is really to become a site of class transformation for first-year college students, then the middle-class project of that classroom has to function best for poor people and especially for poor black people. Right now it irrefutably does not. To make it so, teachers must challenge the myopic concepts of standard English and academic prose, reject code switching, and embrace code meshing straight from the beginning. Why should we expect anything different than hybrid speech and writing that mixes dialects anyway? And what's so wrong with hybrid discourse? Might it not arguably have some advantages over purer discourses, if there are purer discourses? And if students are eager and willing to accept our instruction, shouldn't we be willing to help them code mesh?

Besides getting to the bottom of racialization, the major hurdle, of course, is to get academic institutions and the larger society to call a halt to the moratorium on BEV. This is important because teachers who are eager to accept a proposal like code meshing will continue to feel constrained by institutional and societal beliefs and expectations. Fortunately, however, there is a move in writing textbooks and curricula to privilege the integration of diverse language habits within the standard lingua franca.[3] This should help institutionalize code meshing and provide strategies to implement it.

Until then, teachers like Harley, Cannon, Canagarajah, and me, who function as agents of an educational system that means to sustain and not change or even add BEV to the standard lingua franca, will continue to experience intra- and interpersonal conflict. We'll continue to disagree about whether to change the system or help a few students to navigate it. We will also continue to be ambivalent about whether to condone BEV or condemn it. And, worse, we will continue to be involuntarily oppressive of those who speak BEV, particularly those who personify or speak it to a greater degree than others. These are students who comprise most of the casualties of literacy. If we follow Diane's advice, we'll continue to require the impossible from them—that they save themselves.

Postscript

I can think of no better way to end this chapter than to call readers' attention to a scholar who has shifted from using code switching as a teaching strategy to advocating for code meshing. In his 2006 article "The Place of World Englishes in Composition: Pluralization Continued," A. Suresh Canagarajah borrows and enlarges upon my term *code meshing* (see chapter 4, n9, and Young 2004, 713n9). He writes that code meshing allows for the integration of diverse varieties of English in academic writing. Referencing his 1997 study, which I critiqued in this chapter and in which he required his black students to code switch, he writes, "I have experienced certain difficulties in implementing this approach. I have found that minority students are reluctant to hold back their Englishes even for temporary reasons." He goes on to say that asking students to withhold their dialects from their speech and writing "means 'acting white' for my African American students." And, for students from his native Sri Lanka, he says, it means "putting a show" (2006, 597). Canagarajah is a model teacher who has listened to the voices of his students and has adjusted his pedagogy and teaching ideology so that more of them will succeed. It is my hope that more teachers will follow his example.

TO BE A
PROBLEM

As part of the interview for a professorship at the University of Iowa (hereafter UI), I was asked to give a lecture. I based my talk on the title chapter of this book, using the same autobiographical approach. After my talk the department chair, a man with thirty years in, and who reminded me of a taller, broad-shouldered, fully bearded version of the midwestern farm husband—overalls and all—in Grant Wood's *American Gothic*, asked me only one question: "If you come here, are you going to be a problem?"

His question was loaded, not only because it recalled the question that W. E. B. Du Bois ponders in *The Souls of Black Folk*—"How does it feel to be a problem?"—but also because I'd just narrated the racial conflicts that led to my departure from jobs. What's more, the chair and my prospective colleagues knew of troubles I'd had as a graduate student at the University of Illinois at Chicago (hereafter UIC). Because of the institutional grapevine they knew I had refused to take a required course on how to teach first-year college students to write. They knew I had walked right out of class when I learned that two white students had been given the opportunity to show teaching proficiency by providing a portfolio of their experience. When I asked the director of the writing program for the same opportunity, she gave me the shake-off. Four months later, after much wrangling, when she and her assistant allowed me to submit a dossier, I played what James

Baldwin once called "the bad nigger"—the one who stages his racial and masculine performance to upset white folks (Baldwin 1985, 183).

While preparing my dossier of syllabi and assignments, a flash of resentment washed over me. From my mixed feelings of spite and optimism, I included an epigram on the title page, "You can't take my joy, devil," which I had lifted from a Kirk Franklin gospel song. I had intended the phrase to function as an exposé of the racial politics involved in the situation. I wanted them to know they had delayed but hadn't deflated me. The epigram seemed to convey a certain Christian irony: the more the devil beats you down, the more joy God gives you.

How could I know the director was Jewish? Nor could I anticipate she'd read every anti-Semitic statement Louis Farrakhan ever uttered into the word *devil.* At the time I wasn't fully aware of the racist weight the term bore. If I had been, I might have chosen another, less volatile phrase. Needless to say, she was furious. Her assistant cried. And I was barred from teaching writing. I was given literature classes, an assignment that upset other graduate students who didn't want to teach writing. One told me, "You did wrong, got caught, but still managed to steal away the goods." Perhaps they wanted me to tell them the particulars of my reprimand, but I kept quiet.

What I've rehearsed here, however, was public, and the people at UI knew about it. Nonetheless, there I was with my racial past exposed, seeking to be part of a department that had never had any blacks, let alone a black male. In light of this the chair's question jarred me, confused me, and made me wonder: "Is this a trick?" I deliberated: "If I say I won't be a problem, then the audience, particularly the two blacks present, will wonder, to quote a line from Baldwin, 'Is he for real or is he kissing ass?' On the other hand, if I say I will be a problem, I might be perceived as 'difficult,' 'a trouble maker,' 'a hot head,' 'a race monger.'" Hearing Momma's voice tell me I was there to assimilate, not to alienate, I uttered an acquiescent but assertive no. I was humble but confident, flexible yet focused. I meant my no to indicate that I could function as a team player. Still, I felt disingenuous. I couldn't believe that I was standing there lying, kissing white ass to get a job.

Writing this book has given me pause to ponder my response, and this last chapter is my attempt to discuss the question posed to me in relation first to its archetypal version presented by Du Bois and second to language and literacy. I believe the contemporary problem that blacks face is similar to but distinct from the historical problem that Du Bois felt. One obvious distinction, at least between Du Bois's experience and mine, is that Du Bois's white contemporaries only insinuated the question, hinted at it, which prompted Du Bois to be equally evasive—till he wrote his book. I, on the other hand, was asked directly, boldly, and I was obligated to respond on the spot, indicating to me a cultural change in the decorum between the races. Blacks no longer act generally subordinate, and whites no longer hesitate to ask what they most want to know: Will you challenge us, make us think too much about race, claim racial this, racial that, cry prejudice when we treat and speak to you as we do other whites?

The anthropological interest that whites once had in the unique black experience, it seems, is now mitigated by their concern for how that experience will impact them. Blacks also want to know how my performance of race will affect whites' views of them. I argue that the question that Du Bois considered—"How does it feel to be a problem?"—shifted after integration to "Are you going to be problem?" Everything blacks do or don't do, everything we say or don't say and the *way* we do and don't do things and the *way* we say or don't say something is taken as a performative answer to this new question.

Du Bois's *Souls* addresses what the educational anthropologist Signithia Fordham calls "the First Emancipation," a period that began with the fall of "official enslavement" and that ended with the rise of the modern civil rights movement. During this period, Fordham says, "people of African descent were forbidden to 'act white'" (1996, 350). They were unable to engage in the same activities as whites, and when they did, such as getting a college education, they were not accorded the same benefits. This prohibition against "acting white" defined what it meant to be black during Jim Crow and was metaphorized by Du Bois as the "Veil" of separation between blacks and whites. The external function of the "Veil" had an internal effect on blacks. Du

Bois called it "double consciousness," which he famously characterized this way: "One ever feels his two-ness,—an American, a Negro;
two souls, two thoughts, two unreconciled strivings; two warring ide-
als in one dark body, whose dogged strength alone keeps it from being
torn asunder" (1994, 2).

According to Du Bois, legal segregation produced an intense racial schizophrenia in blacks, which they had to vigorously control in
order to escape both legal consequences and the system of sanctioned
vigilantism (i.e., lynching).[1] Even when blacks, like Du Bois, understood themselves to be no different from whites, they were forced,
by condition, to be only black. Hangings, Jim Crow train cars, and
"white-only" establishments reflect some known consequences of
this condition. This is a point that Du Bois underscores in his autobiographical chapter, "Of the Meaning of Progress," in *The Souls of
Black Folk*.

There Du Bois recounts his journey deep into the country of Tennessee in search of a summer teaching job. He found a school. "Josie
told me of it," he says. She was "a thin, homely girl of twenty." Upon
learning his purpose, "she told me anxiously," he reports, "that they
wanted a school over the hill; that but once since the war had a teacher
been there; that she herself longed to learn" (1994, 38). On the day Du
Bois "secured the school," he went to "the commissioner's house,"
along with a "young white fellow who wanted the white school." The
commissioner was amiable, asked them both about their salary requirements and to "stay to dinner." Du Bois was hopeful, happy: "'Oh,'
thought I," he says, "'this is lucky'; but even then the awful shadow
of the Veil fell, for they ate first, then I—alone" (1994, 39). Du Bois's
unequal treatment by the "amiable" commissioner is an example of
what it means to be forbidden to act white despite one's education or
class.

Even though poverty multiplied the destructive effects of segregation for Du Bois's students, they were nonetheless eager to learn. But
it was to no avail. Visiting ten years later, Du Bois describes their sad
outcomes in gloomy detail, which he epitomizes with Josie's case. So
burdened by race and life's responsibilities, "she crept to her mother

like a hurt child, and slept—and sleeps" (1994, 43). In the chapter's conclusion Du Bois asks: "How shall man measure Progress where the dark-faced Josie lies?" He ends ironically: "Thus sadly musing, I rode to Nashville in the Jim Crow car" (45). Juxtaposing his riding Jim Crow to Josie's class victimization stresses that they both were damned by race. This is not to say that Du Bois didn't recognize the differences between educated, middle-class blacks and their less literate, underprivileged counterparts. His "musing" indicates he did. "Musing" draws attention to his intellect and leisure to ponder the difference and later to write his reflections—opportunities that Josie and his other Tennessee students never had. Still, I wonder: Does Du Bois believe Josie is better off dead? Does he read her passing as freedom from the "Veil" to which he remains subject? Du Bois's narrative illustrates the problem of being black that he both felt and bore witness to in the lives of others.

What does it mean to be black after Jim Crow? According to Fordham, blacks transitioned from being denied the opportunity to act white to being "obligated to 'act white' in order to compete with White Americans" (1996, 350). Many blacks resisted this obligation, arguing for the right to maintain their cultural practices and still have the same opportunities as whites. Therefore, the rise of integration was paralleled by the rise of black nationalism, and "two central state systems" arose in one America. These two systems can be better understood as black and white communities, their ways, and their institutions. Of course, it's blacks who suffer from the rivalry between the two.

Fordham writes that this rivalry "compelled" the black high school students whom she discusses in her ethnographic study "to live an improvised life." This performance, she says, results from "imagining oneself as a citizen in two competing state systems" (1996, 45). Because the students couldn't sustain the compulsory performances of these two communities, they were faced, Fordham reports, with "having to choose one as primary and central" (45). While the community they chose gave rewards, the one they refused punished them. Negotiating rewards for racial loyalty and the penalties received for disloyalty has become a central problem of desegregation.

This problem is illustrated in the case of Daria Muse (1999), a student whose reflective essay is included in a college textbook used to teach interpersonal communication skills. Muse writes that during her elementary and middle-school years, "two personalities emerged." She says, "I began living a double life." One was "a tough, hard-nosed 'bad girl'" who lived in what she calls the "urban jungle" of "South-Central Los Angeles"; the other was a "schoolgirl," surrounded by whites "in the heart of a middle-class suburbia." Both subtle and blatant messages from white teachers and the kids in the ghetto compelled Muse to develop these "different personalities" (1999, 40).

"In a roundabout way," she writes, "I was told from the first day of school that if I wanted to continue my privileged attendance in the hallowed classrooms of Beckford [Avenue Elementary] I would have to conform and adapt to their standards." The standards to which Muse refers are interestingly enough not academic but involve dress and language. "Instead of wearing the tight jeans and T-shirt which were the style in South-Central," she writes, "I wore schoolgirl dresses." "I even changed my language," she says. "When asking a question, instead of saying, 'Boy! Gimme those scissors before I knock you up you head!' In school, I asked, 'Excuse me, would you please hand me the scissors.'" Muse's performativity worked in suburbia: "My appearance and speech won me the acceptance of my proper classmates," she writes. But in the ghetto her school personality "became a dangerous liability." So "once I got off the bus," she admits, "I put a black jacket over my dress, I hardened my face, and roughened my speech" in order to fit in (1999, 40).

What makes the two sites that Muse describes so hostile toward each other? It's that we mark these sites racially and think of them as diametrically opposed. Muse's overstressed rendition of black and white behaviors and language mimics the exaggerated racial perceptions that we have of black and white people. These are perceptions that schools and teachers perpetuate. Even the textbook writers, Ronald B Adler and Neil Towne, endorse Muse's example as one that shows "a wider repertoire of behaviors, the ability to choose the best behavior for a given situation, and skill at performing that behavior" (1999, 40). Because the obligation to perform is required and so pervasive, it has become a part of common sense when it shouldn't be. Even those who are most burdened are inclined to accept it. "I don't regret displaying contrasting behavior in the two different environments. I did it for survival," Muse says. "I act one way in school, which is different from the way I act with my friends, which is different from the way I act in religious services." She continues, "We all put on character masks for our different roles in life." "The trick," she concludes, "is knowing the real you from the characters" (40).

Muse and the textbook writers believe she is expressing a solution when really she's performing the problem. Who is the real Muse? Is she the black ghetto girl she hides at school? Or is she the white suburban girl she hides in the ghetto? If both are fake, then there's no real Muse. If both are real, then behaviors constitute identity and there is no character to play. Contrary to Muse's belief, race is not a role. It's a mistaken legal concept that precedes her existence and determines her identity. Because behaviors are believed to reveal this identity, performance can be understood as a way to conceal it. This understanding of race is what makes it possible for blacks to be obligated to act white or to refuse to do so. Muse dramatizes the racial schizophrenia that segregation forbade but that integration now requires. This burden of racial performance, while not exactly new, is a product not of Jim Crow segregation but of its end. It was precisely desegregation that made the burden manifest, made it heaviest, in fact, where the burden of race should have come undone, in the very site that instigated the collapse of Jim Crow in the first place—school.

My understanding of how school intensifies the burden of racial performance often leads me to say, much to Momma's dismay, that race is still the culprit behind our problems. Momma replies that I risk resurrecting the burden of legal separation, one she experienced while growing up in the 1950s in Yazoo County, Mississippi, and wants to forget. I tell her that what mattered then isn't the same as what matters now. With the end of Jim Crow and with the rise of opportunities to become middle class, the problem for people like me is not whether I'm black or not; everybody knows I'm black. Hell, most of the jobs I've had, even the one at UI, required that I be black. What matters now is what kind of black person I am, which I must demonstrate by the brand of blackness I perform through my speech and behavior.

Momma continues to chastise me, just as some older blacks criticize those of younger generations for circumstances over which we have limited control. Fordham suggests why this is so. She says that many parents born during Jim Crow are ill equipped to help their children manage the racial problems that they face. They "do not understand nor do they see," she continues, "the problems their children see and with which they must contend on an ongoing basis." They "do not fully appreciate just how actively their children are engaged in both creating and maintaining a racialized and culturalized identity" (1996, 350).

The experiential distance between Momma and me has complicated our interactions. Before my job interview at UI, for instance, she warned me, as she always does when I'm to associate with whites, not to talk about race. When I told her it's what I teach and therefore unavoidable as a topic, she asked, "Didn't you used to like Shakespeare?" She believes that I harp on race and consequently will miss out on opportunities that my education should provide. Sometimes Momma reminds me of folks like Bill Cosby and his supporters—very smart, well meaning, but who believe that the black have-nots are to blame for not having much. Momma doesn't see me exactly as a have-not. I have too much education. She is afraid, however, that if I blame too much on race, I won't realize my full potential. This is also a view that some hold about the have-nots. This view isn't entirely the result of a generational difference. Many folks my age believe it too. Older blacks, however, are the ones I hear defending it the most.

Henry Louis Gates Jr., arguably the most influential scholar of black studies, for instance, is one of them. In his *New York Times* op-ed piece, "Breaking the Silence" (2004a), in which he supports Bill Cosby's diatribe against the black underclass, he asks: "Why the huge flap over Bill Cosby's insistence that black teenagers do their homework, stay in school, master standard English and stop having babies?"[2] According to Gates, "Cosby was only echoing sentiments widely shared in the black community" and therefore was saying nothing we haven't heard before. To prove this Gates reminisces about "growing up in the 50's," when he regularly heard comments like Cosby's from his father. Recalling one of those teaching moments, Gates writes: "'If our people studied calculus like we studied basketball,' my father, age 91, once remarked as we drove past a packed inner-city basketball court at midnight, 'we'd be running MIT'" (2004a, A11).

Gates's father recognizes that the problems of segregation and desegregation are not exactly the same. The problem lies in what he makes of the change. To him, because the "Veil" had been ripped, race is no longer a barrier to blacks' gaining education to better their circumstances. If we don't get the gold we desire, then the fault lies not in racism but in our not digging diligently enough for it. This is why he differentiates between blacks who are playing late-night ball in the ghetto and those blacks, like his son, who eventually help lead Ivy League institutions. According to this logic, all blacks have to do to benefit from integration is to work on increasing their class, not performing their race. But Gates's father, and also Gates himself, betray this logic and make performing your race, at least conceptually, of prime importance.

Gates says his father "convinced" his two sons "that the 'blackest' thing that [they] could be was a doctor or a lawyer" (2004a, A11). By persuading his sons that education will make them black, Gates's father is attempting to redefine the site of racial authenticity. The father's concern about middle-class and poor blacks links racial identification—what it means to be truly black—with class identification—and makes it possible for Gates and his brother to reimagine ghetto blacks as less black. He makes middle-class blacks the authentic blacks, the race to emulate. But this is just as irrational as the prevailing logic of authenticity that it seeks to defy. Just as it's now foolish to believe that whites and blacks have a racial essence that makes them biologically different, it's even more ridiculous to displace that essence onto blacks of different classes. This peculiar logic, however, has apparently had a lasting affect on Gates, who uses it to distinguish between famous black historical figures and black and white language.

He writes that while his brother and he "admired Hank Aaron and Willie Mays, [their] real heroes were people like Thurgood Marshall, Dr. Benjamin Mays and Mary McLeod Bethune" (2004a, A11). If all these figures broke racial barriers and are black heroes, why does

Gates subordinate Aaron and Mays? Because they broke racial barriers in sports, Gates associates Aaron and Willie Mays with ghetto blacks, who supposedly sacrifice brains for brawn. Because Marshall, Benjamin Mays, and Bethune broke barriers in law and education, he associates them with middle-class blacks, who supposedly cultivate the life of the mind. Following his father's thinking, Gates has made middle-class blacks the site of authentic blackness and, in turn, has to blacken up school, the site that demands that blacks act white. If he didn't blacken up school, he'd have to come up with a reason other than self-sabotage for why the black underclass fares worse educationally and economically. The conflict about language actually exposes where the problem lies. In support of Cosby's criticism of black youths' speaking BEV, Gates writes:

> Mr. Cosby got a lot of flack for complaining about children who couldn't speak standard English. Yet it isn't a derogation of the black vernacular—a marvelously rich and inventive tongue—to point out that there's a language of the marketplace, too, and learning to speak that language has generally been a precondition for economic success, whoever you are. When we let black youths become monolingual, we've limited their imaginative and economic possibilities. (2004a, A11)

The way I see it, the people who complain most about BEV speakers' growing monolingualism are the very ones who demand it. Influential educators like Gates may acknowledge the "marvelous rich and inventive tongue" of BEV, but they still see it as foreign and different from the "language of the marketplace." It's their beliefs that force BEV not into extinction but into further distinction. Many educators and policy makers may not want to face it, but the linguistic division that they require is the real reason that fewer members of the black underclass have a mastery of standard English. The linguists Joshua Fishman and Ericka Lueders-Salmon made this point more than thirty years ago when they wrote: "The speaker of Black English [is heard as speaking] an outcast's variety as soon as he steps across the boundary of the ghetto. Since many black students are aware of the fact that their dialect is not accepted in the white community, one can in turn understand their growing hostility toward Standard English and their growing ideological defense of Black English" (1972, 72–73).

What Gates recognizes as BEV speakers' monolingualism is not a consequence of their opposition to education but results instead from the linguistic and racial alienation they experience in school. Fishman and Lueders-Salmon predicted exactly what has come to pass: if antagonism against BEV continued, "the black and white verbal repertoires would become even more discontinuous, linguistically and functionally, than they are today [in 1972]" (80–81). And, because they saw language division as a reflection of segregated race relations, they further anticipated that "such discontinuity would not only reflect the social distance between blacks and whites but it would further reinforce and extend this distance as well" (80–81). Too many blacks from the upper and middle classes, and some from the underclass, ignore these linguists and wrongly believe Cosby and Gates. It's easier, it seems, for these people to blame the black underclass for disassociating from school than it is to account for the different role that race has taken in our lives. To offer such an account would require that we take a good, hard look at ourselves, at the way we perform race and why, and require others to do the same.

Because literacy is so important to the lives of black people, I advocate for a concept like code meshing to govern our assumptions and ideologies about language. It may help close some of the distance between the races and might also help address the literacy crisis. If we embrace code meshing, our perceptions of standard English would have to change. The way we use language may not have to change so much, but how we view it definitely will. If we don't embrace code meshing or something like it, the separation of the languages and the races will continue. And not only that: the interpersonal conflict between blacks and the intrapersonal conflict within individual black people will remain. If the examples that I've discussed here or my personal case haven't been persuasive in this regard, then perhaps this last one will be.

In his essay "The Human Contact Zone," written and published when he was a college freshman, Marcus Gilmore says he grew up in a "dilapidated, predominantly black, working class area" (2003, 129); he's "not a great basketball player," and rap is not his "favorite genre of music" (126). Like me, he draws specific attention to his "internal struggle." He says within him is an "internal contact zone" that he negotiates by "acting as a social chameleon" (130). This "contact zone" refers to Mary Louis Pratt's famous 1990 speech in which she used the phrase to define the public space where cultures and racial groups grapple with each other. For many blacks this grappling is a fight for linguistic expression between the inner racialized white self and the racialized black. "When interacting with friends of other ethnic and cultural backgrounds," Gilmore writes, "I make sure my speech patterns model theirs." When talking to whites, he speaks as they do. When talking to black people, he says, "I let my accent slip naturally into urban African American dialect" (2003, 130).

Gilmore is, of course, describing his facility with code switching. It is a practice that may bring benefits but that certainly breeds trouble. Because of the way he speaks, he says, "many whites perceive me as intelligent or as 'one of the good ones.'" Some even think he comes from a "wealthy family" or a "European country" (2003, 129–30). The perceptions that Gilmore says whites have of his speech reveal just how much language is racialized and classed. In relation to those blacks who might speak BEV, Gilmore is seen as "intelligent" and "good," implying what is commonly understood—that BEV speakers are seen as dumb and bad. Further, it's interesting that Gilmore's not perceived to be of African descent but to have a European accent, which Americans adore. By the end of his essay, however, he acknowledges that code switching is just too much and chooses the language and identity he believes will bring him the most benefits. "I no longer routinely try to alter my speech to display my 'blackness,'" he writes (131), suggesting he'll speak only white.

Folks like Gates and Cosby applaud Gilmore's choice; others might attack him. I'm not so much concerned with his decision as I want to point out that he's forced to make an impossible one. As his essay closes, Gilmore recognizes that his problem is not settled and that he's not alone in his experience. Writing about other black males, he says, "We all carry the contact zone within us" (2003, 132). No matter what decision he chooses, Gilmore and his peers have no choice but to be problems.

Of course, I'm also a problem. This chapter, yes, this whole book, has been a reflection on the circumstances that make me one. The chair's question that prompted this final rumination indicates that he too recognizes that I was born into a racial dilemma. After my talk he told me that he'd fully expected me to say, "Yes, of course, I'm going to be a problem." He said that's why he wanted to hire me. He said his question was an attempt to show his unyielding support for my self-reflexivity and that he saw my work as intricately connected to the highs and lows of my academic history. He offered me the opportunity to continue that work at UI, if I desired. Of course, he might have also been saving face for embarrassing me, as one of my colleagues later suggested. But at least everybody knows from the chair's question, my response, and now this book that when it comes to matters of race, I don't submit to the status quo just to make white folks or black folks comfortable.

I've been at UI for four years—the longest I've kept a job, and, to be sure, it hasn't been perfect. I haven't had the opportunity to teach many black students, not a single black male, and, recently, only two black females. But UI accepts 50 percent of its student population from Iowa and the number of blacks in this state is growing. Actually, since I moved here, some members of my family have done so as well, as part of housing relocation programs and Section 8 housing opportunities. They're coming with their children from the ghettoes of Chicago, trying to better their lives. They're bringing with them their BEV and their ghetto ways, as I brought mine. I think about them when I get exasperated with trailblazing. I can't wait to see the younger generations, my family, enter the doors of UI. I believe I'm here to be a problem so that when they come to college, they won't have to be.

postlude
The Street

I'm not of the street, but I grew up on it, experienced terror—even virtue—in its midst, and witnessed enough injustice executed within and upon it to be both cautious and suspicious when police, especially white ones, come running up behind me, asking, as they recently did on a cold Saturday in February, "Can we talk to you?" Eyeing my surroundings on the campus where I teach, seeing no evidence of crime just committed, nor any emergency demanding my attention, and thinking only—at 8 o'clock in the morning—of sending this manuscript to my publisher before heading to the dentist, I declined their invitation and kept on walking. The officers, however, blocked my path and shifted from request to demand, "Stop and show us your identification!" Perturbed by their rudeness and afraid because no one was there to witness their treatment but still aware of my rights, I asked, "What for?" After being told of an anonymous tip, of an alleged warrant for the arrest of a suspect whose age, gender, and race I matched, I asked, "Will any black man do?"

This episode is just one of the too-often, too-many, unjustified encounters that criminalize black men. Unprovoked police interrogation of black men occurs so frequently that the act has become a familiar theme in our cultural discourse. The rap artist Chamillionaire, for instance, in his recent hit "Ridin' Dirty" (2005), tells of a black man who drives a stylish ride, plays loud music, and who is routinely stopped by police because they expect to find "plenty of the drank and dro" in his car. In other words, as Chamillionaire puts it, "They tryin' to catch me ridin' dirty." When he charges racism, he says, "[They] steady denyin' that it's racial profilin'." In my case I too complained of racism, of racial profiling, and the officers, even the chief of police, aggressively denied it.

But I'm not repeating my encounter to argue that I was indeed subjected to the serious but now too easily dismissed act of racial profiling. Nor do I wish to make the case that what happened to me was more egregious than DWB (driving while black) since I was walking not driving. Nor shall I make a point that, according to the Iowa City Police Department's daily log, they should have been looking for someone described as heavyset, not for someone, as Momma puts it, "too skinny for his own damn good." To end with these details would be both redundant (we know the scoop) and reductive. Rather, I cite my experience to go beyond the pedestrian view that I'm a PhD who became just another nigger on the street. Instead, I want to situate my experience in the acts of literacy that took place around the event. Specifically, I want to underscore how literate practices intensify the burden of racial performance, what I've described as the relentless pressure to perform the ultimately futile task of proving the kind of black person you are.

I sent a grievance to the Iowa City Police Department in the same spirit that I've written this book: primarily to draw attention to matters that negatively impact those from the black underclass since they're the ones largely targeted, disregarded, and misrepresented. I received a one-sentence response from Samuel Hargadine, the Iowa City chief of police, saying that my case had been reviewed and administratively closed. I wasn't surprised. I didn't think an entity that investigates itself would openly admit such a big fault. That my complaint is officially on file is enough for me.

I was shocked to learn from a local reporter, however, that Hargadine had released to the press and published on the city's official Web site a rather longish statement about my recent driving record. He revealed that my driver's license was suspended at the time (which, by the way, is why I was walking and not driving) and that I had filed two other racial profiling complaints. Because of this, he said I lacked what he needed to pursue the matter—credibility (see McKanna, 2006, 2A).

The details of Hargadine's forceful skepticism characterize me as a criminal on one hand and as someone who makes frequent and frivolous racial complaints on the other. It's important, however, to consider what he leaves out. The first complaint was in association with a traffic ticket. It was filed with a totally different police department in Cedar Rapids, a city about thirty miles away. The Cedar Rapids police may have ruled out racial profiling, but after I told the judge the circumstances surrounding the ticket I was given, she ruled in my favor. The second case wasn't a complaint but a conversation I had with an Iowa City police supervisor. I wanted to know whether it was appropriate for the officer who stopped me for having expired license plates to also ask where I was going, where I was coming from, where I worked, and why I was driving through a specific neighborhood. Now, even if the first two complaints that I filed were considered unfounded, does that mean Hargadine should have disregarded the third that came to his attention? Is there a limit to the complaints one is allowed to file when one encounters questionable racial behavior from police? Or should all grievances from citizens be taken seriously? But even this isn't what's most disturbing.

To phrase as questions the really crucial point as it relates to education and literacy, I ask: If a college professor's claims about racial profiling are summarily dismissed, what will be the outcome of a complaint from the brotha on the corner, the homie from the hood, or the home girl from the street? If my credibility was challenged by a city official on the basis of the number of complaints I filed, would that encourage others to fight injustice or shy away from public conflict?

To go further, I've heard it said to black students from the hood that the best antidote to racism is an education. But such a phrase actually reveals the burden it imposes. It suggests that the more literacy blacks acquire, the more we'll be exempt from racism. Well, you can't get more literate than to take the PhD in English. Nor can you get more educated than Dr. Antwi Akom, a professor of ethnic studies at San Francisco State University, who was arrested on his college campus after a security guard became suspicious because Akom was in a campus building late one evening (see J. Jones, 2005). His experience occurred just four months before my wintertime encounter with Iowa City police.

I am not saying all this to lessen the importance of literacy. That would directly contradict my life's work. I say life's work because by age seventeen I had already established and was directing a literacy center in the ghetto where I grew up. I was even interviewed by the influential journalist Paula Zahn about the work. So what I'm saying is this: Literacy is not chiefly about matching pronouns with the right antecedents or comprehending why Willie and Janet went up the hill. Literacy is first and foremost a racial performance. Take the code-switching ideology I've discussed and that informs most speaking and writing instruction. When we ask black students to give up one set of codes in favor of another, their BEV for something we call more standard, we're not asking them to make choices about language, we're asking them to choose different ways to perform their racial identities through language.

As I've said, I'm not in favor of sustaining the strict differences between the languages, which is why I advocate code meshing and linguistic integration. We actually code mesh when we communicate anyway. Most everyone comingles vernacular and standard language. But as long as the vernacular and standard remain ideologically reified, racially distinct, then we have to deal with the consequences. And there are several: The more you adopt standard language, the more literate you become, the more educated you appear, the more you're expected to perform and hold ideologies that separate you from the black underclass. And many middle-class blacks and those of us from the lower class who have raised our class status are all too eager to participate in this performative disidentification. We think it will protect us from affronts like racial profiling, as if it's right that any group is profiled. What's more, blacks aren't the only ones to impose this burden on other blacks; whites impose it on us as well. In my experience whites are often shocked and afraid when middle-class blacks hold affiliations and share sensibilities with the lower class. I can't offer a better example than the one I present in chapter 2 of Leanita McClain, the young, successful Chicago journalist who committed suicide. Among other factors, the role of both blacks and whites in enforcing the burden of racial performance caused her to give out.

To return to reactions to my complaint, I should say that of the six or seven older black colleagues I have at UI, only two said anything about the very public incident. One was outraged; the other said, "Forget about it. You know how they do us all. It's best just to go on and show them up with your success." This is another version of the "best antidote to racism" adage. It's posing education as a strategy for emotional and psychic relief. But this relief should come from righting what's wrong, from alleviating the circumstances that caused the trauma in the first place. The circumstances that my colleague unwittingly suggests I change are (1) the color of my skin; (2) my gender; and (3) my racial performance. I say this because if we "know how they do us all," why allow it to continue? What good is our education if we can't use it to fight injustice for ourselves and on behalf of others? Our requiring black people to perform to meet white standards is why some members of the black underclass accuse middle-class blacks of promoting racial disidentification or accuse them of acting white. Even though I've been accused of it myself, there are valid reasons for the assessment. In short, literacy breeds complicity.

Another aspect of "how they do us" pertains to masculinity and sexuality. Historically and today, to justify the excessive efforts used to control and police black men, our language and racial behaviors are misconstrued as hypermasculine. To illustrate, note how often black verbal behavior is called aggressive and how often whites feel threatened by our linguistic styles. As an example, in his statement about me, Chief Hargadine reported that I was speaking loudly and gesturing "animatedly," behaviors taken as threatening to the officers. Officers involved in Akom's arrest described him in the same way. What they refuse to acknowledge is that being accosted by police is not a pleasant experience. It's highly distressing. And it's aggravating to explain your innocence when you're just plain tired of being harassed. How could you not speak loudly when your blood pressure rises? In Akom's case his kids were in the car. I can't imagine that he would speak in hushed tones.

But more than all this, we can't ignore the fact that black men are feared. When we speak out, we could lose our jobs and, worse, our lives. This explains why Momma, even today in the twenty-first century, wishes I wouldn't take jobs in predominantly white towns and schools. This is also why some black men practice speaking in lower registers and are hyperconscious of their gestures and performance. For this same reason, however, some men test just how equal our society is by speaking out freely instead of shape shifting. But we know the cost. It seems that unmanliness is part and parcel of success, even if there are exceptions.

Schools actually teach and breed unmanly performances or, at least, promote white feminine linguistic styles. Note how this is so in Cedar Rapids, Iowa. For a short time I served in that town as a substitute reading teacher to earn extra money. I was responsible for teaching the Read Naturally program to second- and third-grade boys. Read Naturally is similar to Hooked on Phonics. The program has a wide range of stories that are recorded by a female actor. To increase fluency and flow in reading and speaking, students are required to read aloud with the actor, following her rhythm and pace, pronouncing the words as she does. The concept is fine. Good fluency is important to mastering verbal skills and oral expression. The problem is that the recorded reader sounds like a middle-aged white female. Thus literacy is again being associated with a specific gender and race. This association, as I mentioned in chapter 4, is why researchers believe boys many times feel left out during literacy instruction. When this happens, they can't learn the skills that would make them the best readers, speakers, and writers they could be if literacy instruction were more diverse.

Learning to speak and act like a white woman might bring certain benefits. Police officers certainly don't profile them or treat them nearly as offensively as they do black men. But how many black males can or will acquire this performance? Why should we have to? And what kind of animosity will it breed among blacks? Indeed, what kind of trouble does it cause between males who might naturally have a more feminine affect and those who resist these performative requirements by flaunting their masculinity? A postlude isn't the space in which to answer these remaining questions, but asking them promotes more dialogue. And I certainly hope more is said about what I've covered in these pages.

Now that I've posited my piece, I want to end with my last two cents: It's all too simple to continue to believe that black folks from the lower class are self-victims who want nothing out of life. Nothing could be further from the truth. The problem is that the options for getting the better things are limited by the restrictions of literacy. I have not written this book because I wish for a better future. I desire a much better present. I also sincerely believe that we should stop hating on the playas and start assessing the whole game. If we confront the racial ideologies and performances that undergird our assumptions about language and literacy, this radical change will happen.

notes

Prelude

1. In Iowa one out of every 13 black men is in prison, whereas only one out of every 244 whites is. Iowa has the second-highest incarceration rate for black males in the country (behind Wisconsin). The overall population in Iowa is 93.9 percent white, 2.1 percent black. For a more in-depth discussion of these statistics and the related issues, see Dixon (2005).

2. For a full-length discussion of disidentification as it pertains to the performance of various interconnected dimensions of racial, gender, and sexual identities, see José Esteban Muñoz's fascinating study *Disidentifications: Queers of Color and the Performance of Politics*. The word *disidentify* does not exactly follow Muñoz's insightful usage. My use is intentionally idiomatic.

3. I didn't interview the men in the barbershop or make greater attempts to engage them in conversation because I'm not using the methods of formal ethnography in this project. I don't consider the prelude or any chapter in this book to be ethnography. Instead, I'm borrowing from the nonfiction writer's tool kit when sharing my perceptions and observations. However, even if I were to engage ethnography, I still would feel some hesitation and fear. Thus it's important to call attention to the personal insecurities that hinder me, as I attempt to do. In this regard, I'm thinking of the ethnographer John L. Jackson's disclosure of his

"life-long struggle with shyness" that prompts him to "pretend to be other, more famous anthropologists when [he's] out conducting [his] ethnographic fieldwork" (2005, 24). He even takes on the persona of a superhero: Anthroman. For a more detailed discussion of his methods, see chapter 1 in Jackson (2005).

4. The full title of Eversley's book is *The Real Negro: The Question of Authenticity in Twentieth-Century African American Literature.* It's an elegant treatise on the problem of black racial authenticity. Eversley exposes the consequences of trying to judge whether someone is *really* black or just "imitation white" by reading a set of literary texts from the turn of the twentieth century to the present and analyzing the discourse and culture surrounding them.

5. Although not an autobiography, Eversley's book is an effort to figure out the racial and cultural dynamics of her experience in the barbershop. As she writes, "the idea for [my] book happened in [the] barbershop." After recounting her experience, she ends with a reference to "Hortense Spiller's declarative rereading of [Du Bois's notion] of 'double consciousness.'" Compelled by her experience to figure out what this double consciousness means for her life, she writes of herself in third person: "She began to write" (2004, 80).

6. Quincy Mills is listed as coauthor with Melissa Victoria Harris-Lacewell of the chapter that discusses the black barbershop in Harris-Lacewell's *Barbershops, Bibles, and BET,* a provocative and informative study of black talk and discourse. The chapter in question is titled "Truth and Soul: Black Talk in the Barbershop." Because Mills conducted the ethnography and visited the shop, and because the chapter is written from his first-person perspective, I cite him and not Harris-Lacewell in my discussion for the sake of simplicity (see 277n1 in Harris-Lacewell's *Barbershops, Bibles, and BET* for an explanation of her and Mills's ethnographic methods).

7. The issue of gender and masculine performance is a submerged but significant theme in Kotlowitz's discussion of the brothers' relationship to each other and their struggles in the ghetto. Lafeyette, the older brother, for instance, regularly chastises Pharoah for being too soft. As Kotlowitz writes, "Lafeyette believed he had an obligation to toughen him up. He'd badger Pharoah—sometimes calling him 'fag' and 'punk'" (1992, 76). The connection between literacy and a compromised masculine performance is at play here, as Pharoah is also referred to as a bookworm, a boy who liked school. It's also interesting to note that it's Pharoah whom Kotlowitz describes as often fantasizing about leaving the ghetto and living downtown on the lake, suggesting, as I do, a relationship between class climbing, literacy, and anxiety around mas-

culine performance. Overall, however, Kotlowitz represents the boys as having masculine performances that are adequate to move about and negotiate the ghetto. I, on the other hand, did not develop such mobility.

8. Citing feelings of racial displacement and the desire to belong to some racial world is a trope in African American autobiography by males striving toward or born into the middle class. I am thankful to Bridget Harris Tsemo for bringing this to my attention and pointing out the relation between my take on not being black enough to the following statement by Jake Lamar in his *Bourgeois Blues: An American Memoir:* "A black friend once said, 'You're too white for black people and too black for white people'" (1991, 13). For another insightful discussion of this kind of racial liminality, see also Mabry (1995).

Introduction

1. Although the term *Black English Vernacular* and its acronym BEV may appear to be somewhat retrograde in comparison with the more popular term *African American Vernacular English* and its acronym, AAVE, I prefer to use BEV since I use the term *black* and not *African American* to describe myself and the black people I discuss in this book. In this I'm drawing attention to the construction of black (people) in contrast with white (people) and BEV in contrast with WEV. This is purely rhetorical and not a representation of my beliefs about the difference between blacks and whites and BEV and WEV. WEV, of course, is my neo-acronym for White English Vernacular. I prefer this term to the acronym MUSE, which the linguist Rosina Lippi-Green uses for mainstream U.S. standard English. Despite the regional and racial dimensions that Lippi-Green claims MUSE bears, the acronym seems to keep those dimensions hidden and appears to me to be inadequate to foreground and discuss the racialization of language. Therefore, to highlight the racial dimension of standard English vernacular (MUSE) and to point out its arbitrariness as the so-called standard dialect, I refer to it as WEV.

2. Along with E. Patrick Johnson, Bryant K. Alexander has greatly influenced the framework of my project. Not only does his coedited collection *Performance Theories in Education* define "performance as a theoretical lens" (Alexander, Anderson, and Gallegos 2005, 1) and provide useful insights into the way performance can be used to investigate race, but Alexander's stated goal in his article "Performing Culture in the Classroom" does too. In that piece he articulates one of my primary aims: to "engage in the active process of articulating [his and others']

experiences with Black male teachers and other factors that affect [our] educational experience in the predominantly White university" (1999, 322).

3. My use of the term *sociolinguistic* is not meant to suggest that I will conduct a social scientific study of black and white language habits. I use the term in its broad sense to point out the interrelatedness of sociolinguistics to the performance of racial identity. I also intend for the term to call to mind research that I do not cite but that has been influential to my thinking about the performance of raced language and its relationship to academic literacy, for example, Richard Bauman (1977) and Marcia Farr (1993).

4. In Kleinfeld's 1998 report for the Women's Freedom Network she debunks the claim that schools don't serve girls. She argues persuasively that in many respects girls are outperforming boys. Kleinfeld is careful to point out, however, that it is African American boys who are least served by schools.

5. For insightful discussions of the ways whites appropriate black culture and, as a result, further impose a racial burden on blacks that whites themselves do not bear, see Tate (2003). Although I am not making the same arguments as the contributors, the issue of what counts as black and who determines it is important to the general discourse on racial performance.

6. In her groundbreaking essay "Performing Writing," Della Pollock theorizes that performative writing "collapses distinctions by which creative and critical writing are typically isolated" (1988, 80). My performative writing in this volume intentionally seeks to confound and collapse such distinctions.

Chapter 2

1. The distinction that Rock makes between blacks and niggers sounds like Bellew's distinction, but it's not exactly the same. The difference for Bellew is a matter of race—"You can get as dark as you please," he tells Clare (Larsen 1997, 40), because no matter how dark her skin may become, she is, he thinks, white. (The analogy is of a white person with a tan. No matter how dark she may get, it won't change her race.) That's what it means for Clare not to be a nigger. For Chris Rock, however, the alternative to being a nigger is not being white—it's being black. And blackness for Rock has nothing to do with skin color and neither, of course, does his distinction between blacks and niggers. Rather, Rock's difference is based on behavior, on how one performs his blackness.

2. This, of course, does not include the mainstream success that blacks achieve in entertainment industries and sports, where blackness is celebrated—even lionized and imitated. For an account of why blacks have trouble succeeding in mainstream corporations and educational institutions but not in music and sports, see chapter 9, "The Real Trouble with Black English," in Lippi-Green (1997). See also West (2001a), in which he points out the irony of the popularity and success of black male athletes and entertainers at a time when black men are increasingly being killed and incarcerated.
3. Phillip Brian Harper takes up this discussion of racial passing and its relation to black masculinity in chapter 5, "Gender Politics and the 'Passing' Fancy: Black Masculinity as Societal Problem," in his *Are We Not Men?* (1996).

Chapter 3

1. Some essays and books that take up this discussion are Reid-Pharr (2001), Harper (1996), and Ross (1999).
2. To define the BEV rhetorical technique of "loud-talking," Harper cites the work of two well-known sociolinguists, Roger D. Abrahams (1976) and Claudia Mitchell-Kernan (1972). Here he is quoting Abrahams (1976, 19, 54).
3. The literary critic Stanley Fish satirizes and critiques Summers's weak apology for its display of linguistic ineptitude. See Fish (2002).

Interlude

1. Bill Cosby's controversial speech was not made generally available by the NAACP but since has been published on the Internet. See Cosby (2004) for the copy of the speech that I use to discuss it. For a full-length critical discussion of Cosby's speech and biography, see Michael Eric Dyson's provocative study *Is Bill Cosby Right? Or Has the Black Middle Class Lost Its Mind?*
2. For a full-length study of the educational limitations of *Brown* in the lives of black children, see Pendergast (2003).
3. Fifty years after the historic *Brown* decision, many commentators have agreed that its results have been a mixed bag at best. The reasons for the lack of success are complex and range through a variety of factors, including lack of economic and political influence among blacks, population shifts, and the continued polarization among the races.

Chapter 4

1. In his essay "The *Signifying Monkey* Revisited" Kermit Campbell uses the conflict between the black professor and Malcolm X to illustrate how X's response to the professor was X's attempt to signify "not explicitly on school learning" but "on the elitism (not to mention what the black vernacular community calls Uncle Tomming) of certain black representatives of the academic community" (Campbell 1994, 470). I was led back to Malcolm X's autobiography by Campbell's reading of this scene and wanted to enlarge his interpretation, not only by explaining how the racial, social, and class dynamics that took place between X and that professor were also present in my interaction with Cam but also to point out that language is often the touchstone for the larger conflict between the black underclass, represented by BEV, and the black middle class, represented by what is considered to be school English. For me this scene points up a disturbing fact—that instead of closing the gap between the black underclass and the black middle class, education in general and literary instruction in particular aggravates it.

2. For an extended discussion of how BEV is exemplified by black masculine street personalities and how using school English appears to endanger a black man's personality, see Phillip Brian Harper's discussion of the homophobia that is present in African American discourse (1996, pt. 1:2–38).

3. Janice Hale-Benson claims that "the hierarchy of comfort in traditional classrooms is as follows: white females, Black females, white males, and Black males" (1986, 170–71). This strikes me as a terrific basis for arguing that it's time to take the traditional classroom apart and put it back together.

4. Smith's experiences are also narrated in the introduction of his doctoral dissertation, "A Rhetoric of Mythic Proportions: Rhetorical and Trickster Consciousness and Their Effects on Contemporary Society" (2003). The trickster consciousness refers to the way in which an individual *performs* different "ethnic" identities that correspond to particular contexts. See the main of his dissertation for more.

5. In her ethnographic study of "high-achieving and underachieving" black males, Signithia Fordham reports that in order to prove to her "that they were real men, the high-achieving males alleged that they frequented 'sex shops' as part of their regular after-school routine" (1996, 27). In contrast to the high achieving males, "no underachieving male indicated that going to the sex shop or pornography store was a typical part of his after-school routine," Fordham writes (348). This suggests that there is a compelling need in some black communities

for black men who want to achieve academic success to prove their masculinity through sexual, and many times demeaning, chauvinistic, and patriarchal, encounters with women. It also shows that some boys and men who excel academically fear being perceived as less masculine. Therefore, they make conscious efforts to secure their masculinity through rituals of gender performance.

6. Holmes's position is restated in a slightly revised form in chapter 6, "The Rhetoric of Black Voice: Implications for Composition Pedagogy," of his *Revisiting Racialized Voice: African American Ethos in Language and Literature* (2004). He makes at least a few more concessions for BEV than his earlier article allowed. However, his support for code switching remains, which is essentially what I'm arguing against.

7. To be fair to Keith Gilyard, whose written work and organizational work for both the Conference on College Communication and Composition (CCCC) and the National Council of Teachers of English (NCTE) has done much for black students and race studies in composition, I should point out that the edited volume in which he includes Holmes's piece was originally envisioned as a volume that would challenge the concept of race, which, of course, is one of my aims here. Gilyard writes: "I was inclined initially to demand that the contributors to this volume take a hard materialist turn and link race explicitly to historical formations of racism and economic exploitation. The book then would represent a clearly focused rhetorical assault on the idea of race" (1999, ix). Gilyard's volume both enlarges discussions of race in composition studies and depicts the difficulty of those conversations. Holmes's piece in particular illustrates the seemingly no-win situation that black and white teachers seem to be in when teaching literacy to black students. His essay begs for more research on and theorizing of the relationship of literacy and class in black communities and in schools.

8. Smith is referencing and quoting Lewis Hyde, *Trickster Makes the World* (New York: Farrar, Straus and Giroux, 1998), 45.

9. As I argue in the introduction to this book and discuss in longer measure in chapter 5, code meshing is a better alternative than code switching and the other approaches to framing and teaching literacy to black students that I have discussed in this chapter. Code meshing means allowing black students to mix a black English style with an academic register (much as I do in this book). As the linguist Ronald Wardhaugh writes, demonstrating "command of only one variety of language" is so unusual that doing so "would appear to be an extremely rare phenomenon." "Most speakers," Wardhaugh argues, "command several varieties of any language they speak" (1986, 100). Because these varieties are from the same language and not different ones, they overlap and

share many of the same features. From this point of view, code meshing is more natural. Expecting students to write in a form other than code meshing creates artificiality and promotes black student failure in literacy classes. However, treating code meshing as if it were the solution to a racial problem that extends beyond the boundaries of the classroom will only exacerbate the predicament we're trying to eradicate.

Chapter 5

1. Graff gives his source for the Larry material as William Labov, "The Logic of Nonstandard English," in *The Politics of Literature: Dissenting Essays on the Teaching of English,* ed. Louis Kampf and Paul Lauter (New York: Random House, 1972).
2. The writing ineptitude of most corporate workers has long been notorious and recently made the front page of the *New York Times.* According to "What Corporate America Can't Build: A Sentence" (December 7, 2004, 1), "millions of employees must write more frequently on the job than previously. And many are making a hash of it." Reporter Sam Dillon notes that a survey conducted by the National Commission on Writing "concluded that a third of employees in the nation's blue-chip companies wrote poorly and that businesses were spending as much as $3.1 billion annually on remedial training." The tendency to exaggerate the writing competence of middle-class (or even upper-class) white people leads to the prevailing fallacy that they enjoy a higher level of literacy when they don't.
3. See, for instance, chapter 9, "Ain't So/Is Not: Academic Writing Doesn't Mean Setting Aside Your Own Voice," in Graff and Birkenstein (2006).

Chapter 6

1. Reading double-consciousness as schizophrenia comports with the discussion by Gerald Early in the introduction to his edited collection *Lure and Loathing: Essays on Race, Identity, and the Ambivalence of Assimilation.* According to Early, Du Bois used double-consciousness as a double entendre to suggest two uses: as "pure spirituality" or "pure idealism" in a "transcendental" sense, and as "a medical term describing what can be called a '*split personality*'" (1993, xx–xxi; emphasis added).
2. See also Gates's discussion in his follow-up *New York Times* essay on BEV, "Changing Places" (2004b).

references

Abrahams, Roger D. 1976. *Talking Black*. Rowley, Mass.: Newbury House.

Alexander, Bryant K. 1999. "Performing Culture in the Classroom: An Instructional (Auto)Ethnography." *Text and Performance Quarterly* 19:307–31.

Alexander, Bryant K., Gary L. Anderson, and Bernardo P. Gallegos, eds. 2005. *Performance Theories in Education: Power, Pedagogy, and the Politics of Identity*. Mahwah, N.J.: Lawrence Erlbaum Associates.

Awkward, Michael. 1999. *Scenes of Instruction*. Durham, N.C.: Duke University Press.

Baldwin, James. 1985. "Alas, Poor Richard." In *The Price of the Ticket: Collected Nonfiction, 1948–1985*, 269–88. New York: St. Martin's Press.

Bauman, Richard. 1977. *Verbal Art as Performance*. Prospect Heights, Ill.: Waveland Press.

Beaupre, Becky. 2003. "Boys Can't Write: Boys, Not Girls, on Worse End of Education Gap." *Chicago Sun-Times*, March 9, 10A.

Benston, Kimberly W. 2000. *Performing Blackness: Enactments of African-American Modernism*. New York: Routledge.

Bloom, Lynn Z. 1996. "Freshman Composition as a Middle Class Enterprise." *College English* 58 (6): 654–75.

Bonvillain, Nancy. 1993. *Language, Culture and Communication: The Meaning of Messages*. Englewood Cliffs, N.J.: Prentice Hall.

Campbell, Kermit. 1994. "The *Signifying Monkey* Revisited: Vernacular Discourse and African American Personal Narratives." *Journal of Advanced*

Composition 14 (2): 463–73.

———. 1997. "'Real Niggaz's Don't Die': African American Students Speaking Themselves into Their Writing." In *Writing in Multicultural Settings*, ed. Carol Severino, Juan C. Guerra, and Johnnella E. Butler, 67–78. New York: Modern Language Association.

Canagarajah, A. Suresh. 1997. "Safe Houses in the Contact Zone: Coping Strategies of African-American Students in the Academy." *College Composition and Communication* 48 (2): 173–96.

———. 2006. "The Place of World Englishes in Composition: Pluralization Continued." *College Composition and Communication* 57 (4): 586–619.

Chamillionaire. 2005. "Ridin'." *The Sound of Revenge*. Umvd Labels.

Cosby, Bill. 2004. "Pound Cake Speech." Address at the NAACP's Gala to Commemorate the 50th Anniversary of *Brown v. Board of Education*, May 17, Washington, D.C. www.americanrhetoric.com/speeches/bill-cosbypoundcakespeech.htm.

Davis, Thadious. 1997. Introduction to *Passing*, by Nella Larsen, vii–xxxii.

Davis, Thulani. 2002. "Spinning Race at Harvard: The Business Behind the Gates-West Power Play." *Village Voice*, January 16–22. http://village-voice.com/news/0203,davis,31527,1.html.

Delpit, Lisa. 1995. *Other People's Children: Cultural Conflict in the Classroom.* New York: New Press.

Dixon, Bruce. 2005. "The Ten Worst Places to Be Black." *Black Commentator: Commentary, Analysis, and Investigations of Issues Affecting the African Americans*, July 14. www.blackcommentator.com.

Du Bois, W. E. B. 1994. *The Souls of Black Folk.* New York: Dover Thrift Edition. (Orig. pub. 1903.)

Dyson, Michael Eric. 2005. *Is Bill Cosby Right? Or Has the Black Middle Class Lost Its Mind?* New York: Basic Civitas Books.

Early, Gerald. 1993. *Lure and Loathing: Essays on Race, Identity, and the Ambivalence of Assimilation.* New York: Penguin.

Eversley, Shelly. 2004. *The Real Negro: The Question of Authenticity in Twentieth-Century African American Literature.* New York: Routledge.

Farr, Marcia. 1993. "Essayist Literacy and Other Verbal Performances." *Written Communication* 10 (1): 4–38.

Fish, Stanley. 2002. "Say It Ain't So." *Chronicle of Higher Education*, June 21, Chronicle Careers. http://chronicle.com/jobs/2002/06/2002062101c.htm.

Fishman, Joshua A., and Erika Lueders-Salmon. 1972. "What Has the Sociology of Language to Say to the Teacher? On Teaching the Standard Variety to Speakers of Dialectal and Sociolectal Varieties." In *Functions of Language in the Classroom*, ed. Courtney B. Cazden, Vera P. John, and Dell Hymes, 67–83. New York: Teacher's College Press.

Fordham, Signithia. 1996. *Blacked Out: Dilemmas of Race, Identity, and Success at Capital High.* Chicago: University of Chicago Press.

———. 1999. "Dissin' 'the Standard': Ebonics as Guerrilla Warfare at Capital High." *Anthropology & Education Quarterly* 30 (3): 269–93.

Fox, Thomas. 1992. "Repositioning the Profession: Teaching Writing to African American Students." *Journal of Advanced Composition* 12 (2): 291–303.

Gates, Henry Louis, Jr. 1988. Introduction to *The Signifying Monkey: A Theory of African-American Literary Criticism,* xix–xxviii. New York: Oxford University Press.

———. 2004a. "Breaking the Silence." *New York Times,* August 1, A11.

———. 2004b. "Changing Places." *New York Times,* September 30, A29.

Gilmore, Marcus. 2003. "The Human Contact Zone." In *Conversations: Readings for Writing,* ed. Jack Selzer, 126–32. New York: Longman.

Gilyard, Keith. 1991. *Voices of the Self: A Study of Language Competence.* Detroit: Wayne State University Press.

———. 1996. *Let's Flip the Script: An African American Discourse on Language, Literature, and Learning.* Detroit: Wayne State University Press.

———. 1997. "Cross Talk: Towards Transcultural Writing Classrooms." In *Writing in Multicultural Settings,* ed. Carol Severino, Juan C. Guerra, and Johnnella E. Butler, 325–30. New York: Modern Language Association.

———, ed. 1999. *Race, Rhetoric and Composition.* Portsmouth, N.H.: Boynton/Cook.

Graff, Gerald. 2003. *Clueless in Academe: How Schooling Obscures the Life of the Mind.* New Haven, Conn.: Yale University Press.

Graff, Gerald, and Cathy Birkenstein. 2006. *They Say/I Say: The Moves That Matter in Academic Writing.* New York: W. W. Norton.

Hale-Benson, Janice E. 1986. *Black Children: Their Roots, Culture and Learning Styles.* Rev. ed. Baltimore: Johns Hopkins University Press.

Harley, Kay, and Sally Cannon. 1996. "Failure: The Student's or the Assessment's?" *Journal of Basic Writing* 15 (1): 70–87.

Harper, Phillip Brian. 1996. *Are We Not Men? Masculine Anxiety and the Problem of African American Identity.* New York: Oxford University Press.

Harris-Lacewell, Melissa Victoria, and Quincy T. Mills. 2004. "Truth and Soul: Black Talk in the Barbershop." In *Barbershops, Bibles, and BET: Everyday Talk and Black Political Thought,* ed. Melissa Victoria Harris-Lacewell, 162–204. Princeton, N.J.: Princeton University Press.

Henderson, Mae. 2002. Critical foreword to *Passing,* by Nella Larsen, xvii–lxxxv. New York: Random House.

Holmes, David George. 1999. "Fighting Back by Writing Black: Beyond Racially Reductive Composition Theory." In Gilyard, *Race, Rhetoric and*

Composition, 53–66.

———. 2004. *Revisiting Racialized Voice: African American Ethos in Language and Literature.* Carbondale: Southern Illinois University Press.

Holt, Grace Sims. 1972. "'Inversion' in Black Communication." In *Rappin' and Stylin' Out: Communication in Urban Black America,* ed. Thomas Kochman, 152–59. Urbana: University of Illinois Press.

Hoover, Mary Rhodes. 1978. "Community Attitudes toward Black English." *Language in Society* 7:65–87.

Hymes, Dell. 1972. Introduction to *Functions of Language in the Classroom,* ed. Courtney B. Cazden, Vera P. John, and Dell H. Hymes, xi–lvii. New York: Teachers College Press.

Jackson, John L. 2005. *Real Black: Adventures in Racial Sincerity.* Chicago: University of Chicago Press.

Johnson, E. Patrick. 2003. *Appropriating Blackness: Performance and the Politics of Authenticity.* Durham, N.C.: Duke University Press.

Johnson, James Weldon. 1995. *The Autobiography of an Ex-Colored Man.* New York: Dover. (Orig. pub. 1912.)

Jones, Gavin. 1997. "Whose Line Is It Anyway? W. E. B. Du Bois and the Language of the Color Line." In *Race Consciousness: African-American Studies for the New Century,* ed. Judith Jackson Fossett, 19–34. New York: New York University Press, 1997.

Jones, Jessica. 2005. "Black Studies Professor Arrested: Arrest Allegedly Linked to Racial Profiling." *Golden Gate [X]press Online,* October 26. http://xpress.sfsu.edu/archives/breaking/004731.html.

Kennedy, Randall. 2002. *Nigger: The Strange Career of a Troublesome Word.* New York: Pantheon.

Kleinfeld, Judith. 1998. "The Myth That Schools Shortchange Girls: Social Science in the Service of Deception." Report prepared for the Women's Freedom Network, Washington, D.C. www.uaf.edu/northern/schools/myth.html.

Kotlowitz, Alex. 1992. *There Are No Children Here: A Story of Two Boys Growing Up in the Other America.* New York: Anchor.

Labov, William. 1970. "The Study of Language in Its Social Context." *Studium Generale: Journal for Interdisciplinary Studies* 23 (1): 30–87.

Lamar, Jake. 1991. *Bourgeois Blues: An American Memoir.* New York: Summit.

Larsen, Nella. 1997. *Passing.* Ed. Thadious Davis. New York: Penguin. (Orig. pub. 1929.)

Lee, Felicia R. 1994. "Lingering Conflict in the Schools: Black Dialect vs. Standard Speech—Grappling with Ways to Teach Young Speakers of Black Dialect." *New York Times,* January 5, A1.

Lippi-Green, Rosina. 1997. *English with an Accent: Language, Ideology and*

Discrimination in the United States. London: Routledge.

Mabry, Marcus. 1995. *White Bucks and Black-eyed Peas: Coming of Age in White America.* New York: Scribner's.

McKanna, Rebecca. 2006. "Police Chief Backs Officers in Questioning Black Prof." *Daily Iowan,* February 24, 2.

Mitchell-Kernan, Claudia. 1972. "Signifying, Loud-Talking and Marking." In *Rappin' and Stylin' Out: Communication in Urban Black America,* ed. Thomas Kochman, 315–35. Urbana: University of Illinois Press.

Muñoz, José Esteban. 1999. *Disidentifications: Queers of Color and the Performance of Politics.* Minneapolis: University of Minnesota Press.

Muse, Daria. 1999. "Looking at Diversity: Competent Communication in Suburbia and the Inner City." In *Looking Out/Looking In: Interpersonal Communication,* ed. Ronald B. Adler and Neil Towne, 40. 9th ed. Fort Worth, Tex.: Harcourt Brace.

Naylor, Gloria. 1994. "Mommy, What Does 'Nigger' Mean?" In *New Worlds of Literature,* ed. Jerome Beaty and J. Paul Hunter, 344–47. New York: W. W. Norton.

O'Neil, Wayne. 1973. "The Politics of Bidialectalism." In *Black Language Reader,* ed. Robert H. Bentley and Samuel D. Crawford, 184–90. Glenview, Ill.: Scott, Foresman.

Page, Clarence. 1996. "Survivor's Guilt." In *Showing My Color: Impolite Essays on Race and Identity,* 47–69. New York: HarperCollins.

Pendergast, Catherine. 2003. *Literacy and Racial Justice: The Politics of Learning after Brown v. Board of Education.* Carbondale: Southern Illinois University Press.

Pollock, Della. 1988. "Performing Writing." In *The Ends of Performance,* ed. Peggy Phelan and Jill Lane, 73–103. New York: New York University Press.

Pratt, Mary Louise. 1999. "Arts of the Contact Zone." In *Ways of Reading,* ed. David Bartholomae and Anthony Petrosky, 581–600. 5th ed. New York: Bedford/St. Martin's Press. (Orig. pub. in *Profession* 91 [1991]: 33–40.)

Reid-Pharr, Robert F. 2001. "Tearing the Goat's Flesh." In *Black Gay Man: Essays.* New York: New York University Press.

Richardson, Elaine B. 2004. "Coming from the Heart: African American Students, Literacy Stories, and Rhetorical Education." In *African American Rhetoric(s): Interdisciplinary Perspectives,* ed. Elaine B. Richardson and Ronald L. Jackson II, 155–69. Carbondale: Southern Illinois University Press.

Rock, Chris. 1997. *Rock This!* New York: Hyperion.

Rodriguez, Richard. 1982. *Hunger of Memory: The Education of Richard Rodriguez.* New York: Bantam.

Ross, Marlon B. 1999. "White Fantasies of Desire: Baldwin and the Racial Identities of Sexuality." In *James Baldwin Now*, ed. Dwight McBride, 13–55. New York: New York University Press.

Sledd, James. 1973. "Doublespeak: Dialectology in the Service of Big Brother." In *Black Language Reader*, ed. Robert H. Bentley and Samuel D. Crawford, 191–214. Glenview, Ill.: Scott, Foresman.

Smith, Erec. 1999–2000. In Jennifer Cohen et al., "CultureWise: Narrative as Research, Research as Narrative." *Works & Days* 17 and 18:425–43.

———. 2003. "A Rhetoric of Mythic Proportions: Rhetorical and Trickster Consciousness and Their Effects on Contemporary Society." PhD diss., University of Illinois at Chicago.

Smitherman, Geneva. 1977. *Talkin' and Testifyin': The Language of Black America*. Detroit: Wayne State University Press.

Steele, Shelby. 1990. *The Content of Our Character: A New Vision of Race in America*. New York: Harper Perennial.

———. 2002. "White Guilt = Black Power." *Wall Street Journal*, January 8, A18.

"Students' Right to Their Own Language." 1974. Special issue, *College Composition and Communication* 25:1–32.

Tate, Greg, ed. 2003. *Everything but the Burden: What White People Are Taking from Black Culture*. New York: Broadway Books.

Van Der Werf, Martin. 2002. "Lawrence Summers and His Tough Questions." *Chronicle of Higher Education*, April 26, A29–A32.

Villanueva, Victor, Jr. 1987. "Whose Voice Is It Anyway? Richard Rodriguez in Retrospect." *English Review* 76 (8): 17–21.

———. 1993. *Bootstraps: From an American Academic of Color*. Urbana, Ill.: National Council of Teachers of English.

Wardhaugh, Ronald. 1986. *An Introduction to Sociolinguistics*. Cambridge: Basil Blackwell.

West, Cornel. 2001a. "Black Sexuality: A Taboo Subject." In *Traps: African American Men on Gender and Sexuality*, 301–7. Bloomington: Indiana University Press.

———. 2001b. "N-Word." *Sketches of My Culture*, track 6. New York: Artemis Records.

Woodson, Carter Goodwin. 1990. *The Mis-Education of the Negro*. Trenton, N.J.: Africa World Press. (Orig. pub. 1933.)

X, Malcolm. 1964. *Autobiography of Malcolm X*. New York: Grove Press.

Young, Vershawn Ashanti. 2003. "Your Average Nigga: Language, Literacy and the Rhetoric of Blackness." PhD diss., University of Illinois at Chicago.

———. 2004. "Your Average Nigga." *College Composition and Communication* 55 (4): 693–715.

index

Black English Vernacular (BEV)
(*continued*)
some parents to efforts to teach,
2–3; stylistic and rhetorical value
of, 105; viewed as foreign and
different from the "language of the
marketplace," 134
black lower class: accuse middle-
class blacks of promoting racial
disidentification, 143
black lower class, scapegoating of, 69, 78
black males: academic success and
masculinity, 152n5
black male students: choice between
being insufficiently masculine or
insufficiently black, 92, 93; feel
coerced to abandon masculinity
if they succeed in school, 90; feel
forced to abandon their race if
they succeed in school, 90–91;
formation of school-resistant peer
groups among, 4; may be acting
out their own feelings of rejection
by schools, 5; resist most the
performances of race and gender
that schools demand, 4
black masculine performance: and
identifying with the racial concerns
of blacks, 65; and literacy, class,
and anxiety, 148n7; willing
and coerced collusion with
performances that the terms *nigga*
and *faggot* signify, 53, 60
black masculinity: barbershop as site
of, xi, xiii, xiv–xv; and BEV, 90,
152n2; capitalizing on, 61–62;
compromised by academic literacy,
10, 90, 91, 148n7; ghetto masculine
characteristics, 92; narrow
definitions of, xiv; silencing of in
predominantly white contexts,
64–65
black men: criminalization, xii, 139,
147n1; white fear of, 144. *See also*
black professional men
black middle class: defines its class

identity by means of negative
images of lower-class blacks, 69;
ideology, 61; intraracial conflict
with street-identified counterparts,
88
black nationalism, 129
blackness: and concepts of masculinity
and sexuality, 46; as a question
of class, 77; as a rhetorical
performance, 3
black professional men: disidentify
from blackness to escape racism
and to retaliate against black
men, xii; identify with ghetto
to embrace blackness, xii;
performance as compliance with
restrictions on black speech,
65; performance understood
to express homosexuality, 65;
risk of identifying too closely
with the struggles of the people,
66; underplay blackness and
masculinity, 63
black racial authenticity, 45, 133, 148n4;
discourse of, 60; incompatible with
literacy, xvi; and phenomenon of
passing, 42; racial performance as
central problem of, xiii, 37, 49
blacks, transition from being denied the
opportunity to act white to being
obligated to "act white," 129
black students: learning how to write
involves escaping their class and
repudiating the language that
bespeaks their race, 115. *See also*
black male students
black verbal behavior: considered
aggressive by whites, 143;
exaggerated characterization that
could be used as evidence of black
inferiority, 115–16; has become
black person's ultimate sign of
difference, 117; "loud-talking,"
67, 151n2 (Ch. 3). *See also* Black
English Vernacular (BEV)
Bloom, Lynn Z.: "Freshman

Composition as Middle Class Enterprise," 111–12, 114–15
Bonvillain, Nancy, 96
Bourgeois Blues: An American Memoir (Lamar), 149n8
"Boys Can't Write," 4
"Breaking the Silence" (Gates), 132–35
Brown, James, 2
Brown v. Board of Education, 74, 77, 117, 151n3 (Interlude)
Broyard, Anatole, 42

Campbell, Kermit, 4–5, 87, 89, 93; "The *Signifying Monkey* Revisited," 152n1
Canagarajah, A. Suresh: "Safe Houses in the Contact Zone," 118–21
Cannon, Sally I., 113–14
Chamillionaire, 139–40
children, desensitization to violence, 24–25, 34, 35
civil rights movement, 127
class: and academic literacy, xv, 8; apartheid, 74; blackness as a question of, 77; educational guidelines for navigating, 113; and language, 77, 136; and racial identification, 133–34; transformation of in first-year college writing classroom, 121
code meshing, 7–8, 10, 87, 114; allows for integration of diverse varieties of English in academic writing, 122, 142; as a better alternative to code switching, 153n9; and changed perceptions of standard English, 135; defined, 153n9; means abandoning Ebonics, 105–6; within "safe house," 119, 121; subordination of issues of gender and sexuality to race, 8; writing teachers find excuses not to back, 111
code mixing, 7
code switching, 95, 112, 121, 136; informs most speaking and writing

instruction, 142; most teachers still support, 9–10, 105; racially biased, 7; vs. pluralism, 96
college professors. *See* black professional men
composition studies, 153n7
"contact zone," 136
corporate workers, writing ineptitude of, 154n2
Cosby, Bill, 61, 73–79, 132, 134, 151n1 (Interlude)
Cosby, Camille, 78
The Crisis of the Negro Intellectual (Cruse), 32
cross-racial linguistic conflict, 5
Cruse, Harold: *The Crisis of the Negro Intellectual,* 32

Davis, Thadious, 42, 49–50
Delpit, Lisa, 95–96, 98
desegregation, central problem of, 129–31
Disidentifications: Queers of Color and the Performance of Politics (Muñoz), 147n2
Dixon, Bruce, 147n1
double-consciousness, xiii, 128, 148n5, 154n1
Du Bois, W. E. B., 125; notion of double consciousness, xiii, 148n5, 154n1; "notion of the Veil," 115, 127; *The Souls of Black Folk,* 11, 12–13, 125, 127–29
DWB (driving while black), 140
Dyson, Michael Eric: *Is Bill Cosby Right? Or Has the Black Middle Class Lost Its Mind?,* 151n1 (Interlude)

Early, Gerald: *Lure and Loathing: Essays on Race, Identity, and the Ambivalence of Assimilation,* 154n1
Ebonics approach, 105–6
education: "as antidote to racism," 143; guidelines for navigating the American class structure, 113

Elam, William Cecil: "Lingo in
Literature," 116
English, formal, as a gender marker for
women, 91
ethnography, 147n3
Eversley, Shelly, 148n5; *The Real
Negro: The Question of Authenticity
in Twentieth-Century African
American Literature*, xii–xiv, 148n4
*Everything but the Burden: What White
People Are Taking from Black
Culture* (Tate), 150n5

"faggot": association with school and
literacy, 9, 87, 90, 91; avoiding
identity by performing masculinity,
40, 46, 54; black male collusion
with performances that term
signifies, 53, 64; excluded from
authentic "nigga" identity, 57, 60
"Failure: The Student's or the
Assessment's?" (Harley and
Cannon), 113–14
Farr, Marcia, 150n3
femininity, of literary passing subject, 46
"the First Emancipation," 127
Fish, Stanley, 151n3 (Ch. 3)
Fishman, Joshua A., 77, 134–35
Fordham, Signithia, 42–43, 105, 117,
127, 129, 132, 152n5
Fox, Thomas, 83
Frazier, E. Franklin: *Black Bourgeoisie*,
32
"Freshman Composition as Middle
Class Enterprise" (Bloom), 111–
12, 114–15

gang violence, 23–25
Gates, Henry Louis, Jr., 117, 154n2;
"Breaking the Silence," 132–35
ghetto masculine characteristics, 92
Gilmore, Marcus: "The Human
Contact Zone," 135–37
Gilyard, Keith, 98, 111, 153n7; *Voices of
the Self*, 11, 96–97
Graff, Gerald, 106, 154n1, 154n3

Guaman Poma de Ayala, Felipe, 118–19,
121

Hale-Benson, Janice E., 87, 90
Hargadine, Samuel, 140–41, 143
Harley, Kay, 113–14
Harper, Phillip Brian, 5, 46, 63, 66–67,
90, 91, 151n1 (Ch. 1), 151n3 (Ch.
2), 152n2
Harris-Lacewell, M. V.: *Barbershops,
Bibles, and BET*, 148n6
Henderson, Mae, 42, 50
"Heritage" (Young), 17
heterosexuality, performance of, 70,
152n2; in black barbershop, xlv;
home vs. academe, 53–54
Holmes, David G., 4, 93–95, 153nn6, 7
Holt, Grace Sims, 117
homophobia, 152n2
Hoover, Mary Rhodes, 2–3
housing, scattered-site, 26
housing projects, Governor Henry
Horner Homes, Chicago, xv, 8,
17–18, 22–23
"The Human Contact Zone" (Gilmore),
135–37
Hunger of Memory (Rodriguez), 109–10
hybrid discourse, 121
Hyde, Lewis, 153n8
Hymes, Dell, 8

Ice Cube, 48, 49, 60, 61, 62
Ice T., 48, 49
identity. *See* racial identity
*Is Bill Cosby Right? Or Has the Black
Middle Class Lost Its Mind?*
(Dyson), 151n1 (Interlude)

Jackson, John L., 147n3
Jim Crow laws, 7, 9, 115–16
Johnson, E. Patrick: *Appropriating
Blackness*, 3, 10–11, 53–54, 64–66,
75, 149n2
Johnson, James Weldon: *The
Autobiography of an Ex-Colored
Man*, 6–7, 9, 44, 45, 46, 48–49

Jones, Gavin: "Whose Line Is It Anyway? W. E. B. Du Bois and the Language of the Color-Line," 115–16

Kennedy, Randall: *Nigger*, 62–63
Kleinfeld, Judith, 4, 150n4
Kotlowtiz, Alex: *There Are No Children Here*, xv–xvi, 148n7

Labov, William, 91, 106, 154n1
Lamar, Jake: *Bourgeois Blues: An American Memoir*, 149n8
language: ability to acquire, 94; division as a reflection of segregated race relations, 135; effects exaggerating the differences between black and white, 6; equation with class, 136; equation with racial identity, 7, 95, 96, 136; major vehicle for perpetuating the legitimation of oppression, 117; as a performance of gender and sexuality, 5, 54; touchstone for conflict between black underclass and black middle class, 152n1. *See also* Black English Vernacular (BEV); White English Vernacular (WEV)
language prejudice, as an ethical issue, 108–9
Larsen, Nella: *Passing*, 9, 37, 42, 49–50
Lee, Felicia, 105
"Lingo in Literature" (Elam), 116
linguistic dominance, male, 91
linguistic integration, 106, 142
linguistic performance: pedagogy of, 95–96
linguistic segregation, 6, 116
Lippi-Green, Rosina, 43, 75–76, 90, 94, 149n1, 151n2 (Ch. 2)
literacy, of the classroom: casualties of, 105–23; and class, gender, and racial notions, xv, 4, 8, 144; and compromised masculine performance, 90, 91, 148n7; and racial performance, 140, 142;

reproduces the retention problem it's designed to eliminate, 86–87; tension produced for people of color, particularly males, 10
Literacy and Racial Justice: The Politics of Learning After Brown v. Board of Education (Pendergast), 151n2 (Interlude)
Logan Square, Chicago, 18–19
"loud-talking," 67, 151n2 (Ch. 3)
Lueders-Salmon, Ericka, 77, 134–35
Lure and Loathing: Essays on Race, Identity, and the Ambivalence of Assimilation (Early), 154n1

Mabry, Marcus, 149n8
Malcolm X, 88–89, 152n1
McClain, Leanita, 46–48, 49, 50, 143
Million Man March, xiii
Mills, Quincy, xiv, 148n6
minority vs. immigrant, 110
The Mis-Education of the Negro: (Woodson), 45
Mitchell-Kernan, Claudia, 151n2 (Ch. 3)
"Mommy, What Does 'Nigger' Mean?" (Naylor), 62–63
Muñoz, José Esteban: *Disidentifications: Queers of Color and the Performance of Politics*, 147n2
Muse, Daria, 130–31
MUSE (mainstream U.S. standard English). *See* White English Vernacular (WEV)

National Council of Teachers of English (NCTE), 109
Naylor, Gloria: "Mommy, What Does 'Nigger' Mean?", 62–63
"Negro problem," 6
"nigga": association with the hood, 9; black male collusion with performances that term signifies, 53, 64; juxtaposed to "faggot," 60; used to affirm identity and community, 9

"nigger": "bad," as one who stages racial/masculine performance to upset whites, 126; Cornel West's view on use of, 68, 70; positive validation of masculinity, 62–63; as a term distinct from blacks, 37–39, 45, 150n1; used to distinguish "ghetto" blacks, 37–38, 45, 89, 90–91; use of neutralizes racial perspective, 88–89
Nigger (Kennedy), 62–63
"N-Word" (West), 68

O'Neil, Wayne, 113

Page, Clarence: "Survivors' Guilt," 47–48
passing. *See* racial passing
Passing (Larsen), 9, 37, 42, 49–50
Pendergast, Catherine, 151n2 (Interlude)
performance. *See* black masculine performance; heterosexuality, performance of; racial performance
Performance Theories in Education (Alexander), 149n2
performative writing, 150n6
"Performing Culture in the Classroom" (Alexander), 149n2
"Performing Writing" (Pollock), 150n6
"The Place of World Englishes in Composition: Pluralization Continued" (Canagarajah), 122–23
pluralism vs. code switching, 96
Pollock, Della: "Performing Writing," 150n6
poverty, tools for escaping as tools for escaping identity, 101
Pratt, Mary Louise, 118–19, 121, 136

Quecha, 119

race: effects of exaggerating and reifying the differences between, 6; equated with language, 4
race switching, 97–98

racial apartheid, 74
racial authenticity. *See* black racial authenticity
racial displacement, 149n8
racial identification, linked with class identification, 133–34
racial identity: equation with language, 7, 95, 96, 136; racism compels students to give up, 90; and sociolinguistics, 3, 150n3
racial loyalty and disloyalty, rewards and penalties for, 129
racial narrative, as vehicle for making conceptual arguments about language learning, 11
racial passing: as "acting white," 43; and black racial authenticity, 42; femininity of passing subject, 46; Jim Crow saga of, 45; novels, 42; as striving toward whiteness and repudiating blackness, 46; supplanted by racial performance in post–Jim Crow era, 9, 37
racial performance: burden of, 1–13, 37, 92–93; burden of intensified by schools, 129–31; as central problem of black racial authenticity, xiii, 37, 49; demand for reduced by antiessentialism, 50; and literacy of the classroom, 140, 142; often carried out through language, xiii, 7, 140, 142; performative disidentification, 75; pervasive requirement, 3; refusal to enact, 50; reinscribes the essentialism it's believed to subvert, 11; required to achieve success in America's mainstream, 43; and sociolinguistics, 3, 150n3; sociolinguistics of, 3, 150n3. *See also* black masculine performance; black professional men
racial profiling, 139–45
racial schizophrenia, forbidden by segregation but required by integration, 129–31

INDEX / 166

"Veil," 115, 127, 133
vigilantism, 128
Villanueva, Victor, 110, 111, 112;
    Bootstraps, 11; "Whose Voice Is It
    Anyway?", 109
violence, desensitization to, 24–25, 34,
    35
Voices of the Self (Gilyard), 11, 96–97

Wardhaugh, Ronald, 153n9
West, Cornel, 63, 67–69, 151n2 (Ch. 2)
White English Vernacular (WEV),
    90, 149n1; association with a
    white racial profile, 97; and its
    nonstandard vernacular, 100;
    methods that teachers use to get
    students of color to use, 112;
    speaking puts blackness and
    masculinity at risk, 90, 91; vague
    and limited scope of codes used to
    define, 112
whites: comfort with nonthreatening
    black men, 66; concern for how

the black experience will affect
    them, 127; impose performance
    expectations upon blacks, 4
white southern speech, represented in
    print as correct, 116
"Whose Line Is It Anyway? W. E. B.
    Du Bois and the Language of the
    Color-Line" (Jones), 115–16
"Whose Voice Is It Anyway?"
    (Villanueva), 109
Winfrey, Oprah, 63
women, formal English as a gender
    marker for, 91
Woodson, Carter F." *The Mis-Education
    of the Negro*, 45
writing, performative, 150n6
writing classroom, as a site of class
    transformation for first-year college
    students, 121
writing textbooks, move to privilege the
    integration of diverse language
    habits, 122

acknowledgments

I would like to acknowledge

My professors at the University of Illinois at Chicago: Walter Benn Michaels, Ralph Cintron, Dwight McBride, and, especially, Gerald Graff.

My colleagues: Gail Boldt, Aimee Carrillo-Rowe, David Depew, Keith Gilyard, Robert Latham, Cynthia Lewis, Charles Nero, Ifeoma Nwankwo, Elaine Richardson, Carol Severino, Thom Swiss, Mary Trachsel, Victor Villanueva, Doris Witt, and, especially, Venise Berry and Bridget Harris Tsemo.

My family: Dorothy "Momma" Young, Katrina Young, Lakia Young, and especially, Y'shanda Young Rivera.

My friends: Randall Bates, Ollie Calhoun, Johnny Fleming, Skye Frank, Corliss Garner, Cornel Logan, Charline Minefee, Monica Jefferson Mosby, Lisa Smith, Louis Wright, and, especially, Florida Binns.

My research assistants at the University of Iowa: Valerie Nyberg, Wanda Raiford, Adam Roth, Aaron Sachs, and, especially, Amit Rahul Baishya and Ann Pleiss.

My editors at Wayne State University Press: Melba Boyd and Ronald Brown, series editors; Kathryn Wildfong, acquisitions editor; Kristin Harpster Lawrence, managing editor; and a special thanks to Polly Kummel, a copyeditor who reads beyond the surface and with keen insight.

To all of you: The comments you offered me on this text proved invaluable. Although we didn't always agree, our conversations both enhanced my thinking and enriched this book.

Thank you.